His own ha
of her shou
living warm
of her breas
beneath his

As if in s̶o̶ into the bed. He laid her tenderly on the soft, pink bed-cover and swiftly removed his clothes. She had kicked off her shoes and peeled off her tights. Her skirt and blouse were dropped onto the floor and she wore only a wisp of nylon as panties, as she regarded him in his nakedness.

He was about to join her on the bed but first . . .

By the same author

The Happy Hooker
Letters to the Happy Hooker
Xaviera!
The Best Part of a Man
Xaviera's Supersex
Xaviera Goes Wild!
Xaviera Meets Marilyn Chambers (with Marilyn Chambers)
Knights in the Garden of Spain
Xaviera's Magic Mushrooms
Madame l'Ambassadrice
The Inner Circle
Lucinda, My Lovely
Fiesta of the Flesh
Lucinda, Hot Nights on Xanthos
Happily Hooked (with John Drummond)

XAVIERA HOLLANDER

Erotic Enterprises Inc.

GRAFTON BOOKS
A Division of the Collins Publishing Group

LONDON GLASGOW
TORONTO SYDNEY AUCKLAND

Grafton Books
A Division of the Collins Publishing Group
8 Grafton Street, London W1X 3LA

Published by Grafton Books 1986

First published in Great Britain by
Aidan Ellis Publishing Limited 1985

Copyright © Sonvico Trust 1985

ISBN 0-586-06254-8

Printed and bound in Great Britain by
Collins, Glasgow

Set in Baskerville

All rights reserved. No part of this publication
may be reproduced, stored in a retrieval system,
or transmitted, in any form, or by any means,
electronic, mechanical, photocopying, recording or
otherwise, without the prior permission of
the publishers.

This book is sold subject to the condition that
it shall not, by way of trade or otherwise, be
lent, re-sold, hired out or otherwise circulated
without the publisher's prior consent in any
form of binding or cover other than that
in which it is published and without a similar
condition including this condition being
imposed on the subsequent purchaser.

Author's Preface

England has for too long been deprived of the presence of Lucinda, daughter of Gerald Farrer, Viscount Hamblewood, gentle, dotty aristocrat, and his sharp-witted, American wife, Melanie. Without Lucinda, the love life of the country has languished and erotic activity has diminished pathetically.

In LUCINDA, MY LOVELY, I recounted how Lucinda had sexually sabotaged a Cambridge college and then got into (and out of) a French gaol after the murder of a super-pimp. Her subsequent career, as the joint owner, together with her school friend and lover, Jennifer Maxwell, of a call-girl agency in Paris has never been recorded in detail in accordance with the insistence of some of her influential clients.

Then, Lucinda and Co. set out on a voyage which took them to a remote Greek island where they came into possession of a rare and wildly effective aphrodisiac after a duel of wits with Lucinda's rascally uncle, Ulysses. But that story, the sequel to LUCINDA, MY LOVELY, I have narrated in XANTHOS.

Now, we find Lucinda and her friends, sailing back from Xanthos. Can they resist the lure of yet another series of amorous adventures? Can a cat keep its nose out of a bowl of cream or a mouse resist the seductive aroma of cheese?

PART I

'Thy Nobler parts which but to name
In our Sex would be counted shame,
By Age's frozen grasp possest,
From their ice shall be releast:
And sooth'd by my reviving hand
In former warmth and vigour stand.

(Song of a Young Lady to her Ancient Lover)
JOHN WILMOT, EARL OF ROCHESTER

CHAPTER 1

The setting sun was turning the peaks of the Maritime Alps into fantastic, pink sugar-loaves as the ketch, Lucifer, slipped into the shelter of the anchorage of La Napoule. At the wheel stood the skipper, Alain, a Breton ex-fisherman. He was a powerful, stocky youth with crisp, curly, black hair. Jennifer Maxwell was at his side. Dark, sensitive featured, Jennifer was the daughter of a world famous actor. She and Lucinda Farrer owned the yacht and Jennifer was the lover of both Alain and Lucinda.

At the rail, two passengers watched as they approached the theatrical, little French port, Lucinda's brother, Miles and his pregnant wife, Sarah. Miles Farrer was an up and coming barrister who used to regard Lucinda's high spirits and frivolous misadventures with solemn disapproval until he met Sarah. His ash blonde Australian wife had infected him with something of her own natural exuberance and his lectures to his sister on her behaviour had become much less frequent events.

There was the usual flurry of activity as they set to work, berthing the ketch.

'Where the hell are Brian and Lucinda?' Alain demanded angrily. 'They ought to be up here, giving a hand.'

'Where do you think they are?' laughed Jennifer. 'Where do they get to every day at this time?'

There was no mystery. Miles had pronounced his sister a nymphomaniac, Brian, her lover, admitted that she was highly sexed and Lucinda stated simply that she had a healthy appetite. This was the hour which she had declared for the duration of the voyage to be devoted to her 'crew-screw'. So, while the other two were busy furling the sheets aloft, she and Brian were busy filling the sheets below.

When Lucinda had first met Brian, he was a rather untidy, rebellious spirited hitch-hiker. But in the months which followed, he had matured and revealed unsuspected talents and, according to Lucinda, developed into a super-stud. Lucinda lay contentedly in his arms in the vast bed which took up most of the owner's cabin. She was enjoying that excitement which comes from anticipation of good sex.

Lucinda was an outstandingly pretty girl with golden hair and fair skin which had been bleached a tone lighter by the caress of sun and wind as they had sailed back from the Greek islands. Brian lovingly stroked her delicate throat, the subtle slope of her shoulders and the full, rounded ripeness of her breasts and she purred with pleasure. She felt that familiar quickening of her senses, the flowing of her juices and the mounting of sweet desire. She pressed her mouth against his, her tongue questing and teasing him, its probing challenging him to thrust his strong, erect penis into her hungry vagina. Brian held her firmly against him, breathing in the sensual aroma of her body.

'Shouldn't we be on deck, helping Alain bring Lucifer in?' asked Brian mischievously in a voice which made it obvious that he had not the slightest intention of stirring from the bed.

'Your place is here,' replied Lucinda, spreading wide her legs and guiding him into her. 'Let's end the voyage in style.'

Brian kissed her while Lucinda pinched and kneaded

his firm flesh. They moved together in a sinuous, erotic rhythm, rejoicing in the seductiveness of their fine bodies.

'Give it to me, now,' Lucinda moaned.

So, as the yacht bumped against its mooring, they raced to their marvellous climax. Lucinda had closed her eyes in sheer bliss and she felt her whole being shaken by the impact of her orgasm. Brian, as always, came with her – strongly, sweetly, satisfyingly.

'That was great and a lot more fun than bringing a boat into a harbour wasn't it?' Lucinda asked as they basked in the golden afterglow.

By way of answer, Brian kissed her again.

'I wonder what has become of Uncle Ulysses,' Lucinda mused.

'The old scoundrel ought to be behind bars,' Brian commented. 'But you seem to have a sneaking admiration for the black sheep of your family.'

'Well, the old boy did have style.'

'Style!' snorted Brian. 'He threatened to kill the lot of us.'

'I think that he was bluffing,' Lucinda contended. 'He was the most convincing liar I have ever met. Remember all those fantastic yarns he fed us – and we believed every word. I have a hunch that we haven't heard the last of Uncle Ulysses and some day, the old charlatan will slither out of the woodwork.'

'If he does, you had better watch out,' said Brian. 'I don't suppose that he will ever forgive you for robbing him of the heather from Xanthos.'

Brian was referring to erica erotica – a plant which was unique to the virtually unknown island of Xanthos and which, when crushed and its juice distilled, yielded an aphrodisiac of stupendous power. The crew of Lucifer had frustrated the plans of Ulysses and the source of this wonder heather was now safely in their hands.

A short time later, they were all ashore in a waterside café, enjoying the luxury of fresh coffee and croissants.

'I suppose that you will be wanting to get back home to Hamblewood,' Jennifer said to Sarah.

'Certainly,' Miles interposed. 'We have had quite enough dashing all over the world. Sarah should be taking things easy.'

'Nonsense!' his wife contradicted. 'I can carry on for months yet.'

Miles was obviously not convinced and insisted on playing the role of expectant father.

'Why don't the rest of you come along with us?' asked Sarah. 'Hamblewood is big enough to accommodate an army and you could all do with a break.'

Alain shook his head. 'There's quite a lot of work to do on Lucifer. I must stay.'

'And I'll stay with you,' smiled Jennifer. 'You'd get lonely if we left you here on your own.'

'You want to keep your eye on him in case he shacks up with one of the locals,' Lucinda accused.

'You know me too well,' Jennifer conceded. 'But wouldn't you like to go and visit your loving parents, Lucinda?'

'It's not a bad idea. Mummy's away and, given half a chance, Daddy will get into some sort of trouble. What about you, Brian; will you come with me?'

Brian hesitated. He was accustomed to Lucinda in the rough and tumble of life at sea, but he was not sure what she would be like in the surroundings of the stately home where she belonged.

'Do come,' Sarah urged. 'You are a good influence on Lucinda and my hands are full, keeping her brother in order. I couldn't possibly cope with the two of them on my own.'

'And don't worry about our dignified parents,' added Miles. 'In her time, Lucinda has brought home so many strange specimens of humanity that they will be immensely relieved to find her consorting with somebody as pleasant and uneccentric as you.'

Brian was not certain whether he ought to be flattered by Miles' qualified compliment but before he could reply, Lucinda answered for him.

'Fine! So it's settled then. The four of us set off tomorrow as near the crack of dawn as we can manage while Alain and Jennifer stay and look after 'Lucifer'.

Brian smiled and nodded. It was not the first time, nor would it turn out to be the last, that Lucinda had made up his mind for him.

CHAPTER 2

A couple of weeks before the arrival of 'Lucifer' at La Napoule, the sun shone brightly on Hamblewood and spring filled the heart of Gerald Farrer with exultation. His wife was leaving him. Not permanently, he reflected ruefully, but for long enough to bring him a whiff of the heady aroma of freedom.

'Now, do look after yourself while I am away,' cautioned the Viscountess, 'and try to keep out of mischief.'

The Viscount protested feebly, as if he had never journeyed on any other road than the Path of Virtue.

Melanie was about to set out on a six month, lecture tour of her native United States. In the company of the wives of a missionary who dwelt in the forests of New Guinea and of a mining engineer, currently working in Zaire, the Viscountess had agreed to enlighten her audiences on the problems which confront American women, condemned to spend part of their lives in the wilderness, that is to say, outside the United States.

'And for God's sake, dress properly,' was her parting injunction to her spouse. 'Don't go mo333333g about in that disreputable, old jacket. It sets a bad example to the staff and it is a shock for visitors. After all, people pay for admission to a stately home, not a home in a ghastly state. And they don't expect to see a Peer of the Realm, looking as if he had bought his clothes at a charity bazaar.'

As soon as the tyrant who controlled his life had departed, Gerald Farrer, whistling tunelessly a song which had been popular in the twenties, put on a pair of grey, flannel trousers which had seen better days and the offending, shapeless tweed sports jacket with its worn leather elbow patches. He was ready to face the world. And, although he did not yet know it, the world was preparing to meet him. Each moment took his wife further away and the Viscount toddled aimlessly but happily around the stables and the pig-sties, casting a benevolent gaze over his domain. He chatted unknowledgeably with the head gardener. He even went as far as to tell a joke about an Englishman, a Scotsman and an Irishman to the butler who smiled patiently but was clearly not amused. Then, he called for the cook and contradicted all the instructions which Melanie had left. Life was good!

Then, Fate intervened. There was a party of sightseers, ambling around the house, and Gerald took it upon himself, as was his custom, to act as guide and to provide them with a commentary which vaguely approximated to the factual history of the great house. When the tour was over and the rest of the party trooped away, two visitors stayed behind.

The man was middle-aged and thickset. Although clean shaven, his chin had a blue-black tinge which talcum powder could not completely hide. He wore heavy, horn-rimmed spectacles which gave him an air of desperate seriousness. His companion was a well upholstered blonde who had sought to enhance her somewhat over-abundant charms with a deluge of cosmetics and pungent perfume. The man approached Gerald Farrer and extended his hand.

'Sir, it has been a privilege for my friend and myself to have been welcomed by you into your lovely home and I would like to express my gratitude.'

Gerald was taken by surprise. He blushed myopically and found himself shaking his visitor's hand.

'Allow me to introduce myself. I am Hiram T. Watergate from Rhode Island.'

'Watergate?' mused the Viscount. 'The name seems to be familiar but I can't quite place it.'

Hiram shot a meaningful glance at the woman.

'Indeed, sir,' he replied. 'The Watergates are among the few surviving families from the original settlers in Rhode Island. That is a fact which is very little known outside the immediate family circle. But forgive me, I should have presented my companion, the Contessa de Scarpio.'

The buxom blonde nodded haughtily to Gerald and announced,

'Swell meeting you, Viscount.'

The lady's title had led Gerald to expect a foreign accent, reminiscent of the musical lilt of the Italian language. Actually, her voice had the unmistakable twang of New Jersey.

Gerald Farrer never quite understood how it came about, but when he wandered into the library, his two new acquaintances were still at his side, favouring him with their conversation. And it would have somehow seemed churlish and impolite not to invite them to stay for lunch.

During the meal, Hiram disclosed that he was a wealthy businessman, snatching a brief vacation.

'Somehow whatever I touch turns to gold,' he informed his host. 'You can have no idea how embarrassing that can be.'

He was quite right. Gerald Farrer had no idea. The few occasions he had ventured into the world of commerce and finance had proved to be unmitigated disasters. He considered that Hiram T. Watergate might well be a man to be reckoned with and he felt vaguely that a closer relationship with that worthy could turn out to be advantageous.

However, it was the exotic Contessa who made the greater impression on their host. Throughout the meal, she gazed intermittently into his eyes. At length, she observed,

'You know, Viscount, you possess all the fine features of the British aristocracy in your face. When I look at you, I am reminded of a portrait which we have in my family of your Oliver Cromwell.'

One of Gerald's ancestors had fought for King Charles and had fled into exile with his son, but when he looked into the melting, blue eyes of the lady, Gerald had not the heart to object to the dubious compliment.

'Really, my dear Contessa,' he waffled.

'Please, call me Semiramide,' she cooed.

'What an unusual name,' he gushed. 'And you, my dear, must stop calling me Viscount. The name is Gerald.'

By the end of lunch, the trio were firm friends, Hiram

invited Gerald for an evening on the town in London – dinner, a show and a nightclub, but the noble lord declined. He felt that his emancipation had not yet progressed to that extent. But next day, he received a gift from Hiram, consisting of some American cigarettes, a couple of bottles of Bourbon and a porno-video which was unlike anything that Gerald had previously encountered. The cigarettes also seemed to contain something more than unadulterated tobacco.

Hiram and Semiramide became frequent visitors to Hamblewood and it was virtually inevitable that Gerald should reciprocate their enjoyment of his hospitality by inviting them to dinner.

On the appointed evening, Gerald, resplendent in a dinner jacket and black tie, awaited his guests. Presently, Thistlethwaite, the butler, announced,

'The Contessa de Scarpio, milord!'

Semiramide swept into the room. She was wearing a silver lamé dress which had the effect of thrusting her bosom forward, like the prow of an ocean liner. Her hair cascaded over her shoulders and her lips were plastered a vivid scarlet.

'Gee, I am sorry to have to disappoint you, Gerald dear, but Hiram has had a sudden call to London. Some tiresome business or other about some oil wells he owns. It was urgent and he couldn't put it off until tomorrow. He begs you to excuse him. Can you bear making do with me alone? I guess I haven't got Hiram's powers of conversation: you must find me terribly boring.'

'No, not at all! I am sure that we shall get along splendidly,' answered Gerald gallantly. 'Still, I am sorry that Hiram couldn't make it.'

Even as he said the words, Gerald was conscious that he was not being strictly truthful. He would have liked to entertain the dashing Mr Watergate and maybe learn something about such things as oil wells but, for some reason, he felt even happier to have the undivided attention of Semiramide.

The dinner was an undoubted success. The Contessa was enthusiastic over the food and the wine flowed in greater abundance than would have been the case if Melanie had been presiding. After the meal, Gerald was in no hurry to dismiss his guest and Semiramide maintained a gentle babble of conversation which convinced Gerald that she was enjoying the evening.

Later, they were sitting in the Blue Salon, sipping coffee and liqueurs. Semiramide gazed through the tall French windows.

'The gardens look lovely in the moonlight,' she said. 'But from upstairs, the view must be even more spectacular.'

'I suppose so. I've never noticed,' confessed Gerald. 'Would you like to see?'

'Please!'

So, Gerald Farrer led the way up the sweeping, marble staircase and into a spacious bedroom.

'This is a room we keep for guests,' he announced. 'However, it does look out onto the terrace and the grounds, right down to the lake.'

Semiramide favoured the view with a cursory glance.

'But what is it like from your own room?' she asked.

'Oh, I sleep in a much smaller room,' smiled Gerald. 'It overlooks the stables and the kitchen gardens. Nothing there to interest you, I'm afraid.'

'I am sure it is really quite charming,' Semiramide persisted. 'Won't you show me?'

'It's nothing to get excited about,' replied the puzzled peer. 'But, if you are curious. . .'

Gerald shook his head, like a bewildered sheep-dog and ushered his guest along several corridors and into his bedroom.

Semiramide looked out of the window. Then, she seemed to totter a couple of steps and passed her hand over her forehead.

'Forgive me,' she gasped. 'But I suddenly feel rather faint. Do you mind if I lie down for a minute?'

Without waiting for a reply, she spread herself on Gerald's bed.

'Would you like me to go and bring you a glass of water?' Gerald volunteered anxiously. 'Or perhaps some smelling salts? I am sure that there are some in my wife's room.'

'No, no, please, don't bother. Just come and sit beside me until it passes.'

She kicked off her shoes and Gerald perched gingerly on the bed next to her.

'I'd feel better if this dress were loosened. Would you be an angel and help me?'

It would have been ignoble to refuse and Gerald fumbled with the complicated array of buttons, hooks and zips. He got the definite impression that Semiramide was arching her body up to meet his nervous fingers. Perhaps it was only his imagination but certainly without his intending it, he found that his hands kept coming into contact with expanses of warm, yielding flesh.

Finally, Semiramide slithered out of the tight sheath of her dress with an alacrity that suggested that her faintness had given way to a more pressing sensation.

'Oh, I say,' observed the Viscount. 'You are not wearing one of those brassiere things.'

'I find them too constricting,' Semiramide explained. 'I believe that the body should be free. Don't you agree?'

'Er, yes, definitely,' Gerald answered uncertainly.

'Good. Then why don't you slip off your jacket and that bow tie? How can you relax when you are all buttoned up?'

'That's quite all right,' Gerald assured her hastily. 'I am perfectly comfortable.'

'Well, I am not,' retorted Semiramide, as she wriggled closer to him. 'You make me feel so awkward, lying here practically naked while you are so formal. You would not want me to feel embarrassed, would you?'

'Good Lord, no,' Gerald admitted guiltily, as he discarded the offending coat and tie. 'I never thought about it that way.'

He was sitting beside her on the bed and, for some reason which he could not fathom, Semiramide's fingers fluttered around his shirt and trousers and, as if by magic, all his buttons were undone and his body was open to her hands.

A wildly improbable thought began to percolate through Gerald's brain. Tentatively, he stroked Semiramide's shoulders. She did not repulse him, as he had feared, but turned her body towards him so that he found his hands were unexpectedly fondling her full, heavy breasts.

'Oh, Gerald,' she breathed. 'You are so manly.'

'Am I really?' asked the startled seducer.

'May I ask you something personal – very personal?'

'Anything you like,' he replied, throwing caution to the winds.

'There is a tradition in my family,' Semiramide told him coyly, 'that all English aristocrats are circumcised. Is it true?'

'No, no. Perhaps you are confusing us with rabbis.'

'But what about you, Gerald?'

'No, I do assure you.'

'May I look? Just a peep?'

'Do you think that would be proper? I mean to say . . .'

'There's no harm, Gerald, dear,' she interrupted. 'After all, we are old friends, aren't we? And I am so curious.'

Gerald had no opportunity to express his doubts further because Semiramide had twitched off his trousers and pants with an expertise which might have indicated long practice. She regarded his penis as if it were one of the wonders of the world.

'Oh, Gerald,' she murmured delightedly. 'Isn't it sweet? And look, it's getting so big.'

It was true. Melanie never had that effect on him. But Gerald's erection could hardly be termed spontaneous, since Semiramide's fingers were tenderly coaxing him in a manner which his wife would have condemned as most unlady-like.

'I say, do you think we ought – '

But Gerald's objections were stifled as Semiramide pressed her lips against his and thrust her tongue into his mouth. He said nothing since he had been taught that it was rude to speak with his mouth full.

After that, things got a bit confused. Gerald was not quite sure how it was that he clambered into bed with Semiramide and the rest of his clothes were spirited away.

One thing was certain. His guest's giddy spell had vanished. Gerald was lying on his back and her hands seemed to be all over his body at the same time. He was groping at her inviting flesh without much sense of direction.

To tell the truth, Gerald was flabbergasted by the turn of events. He could not recall the last opportunity which had been presented to him for an amorous adventure during his existence under the cold scrutiny of Melanie and, as for his marital love-making, that had been governed by an unwritten code, stricter than any diplomatic protocol, which had excluded anything as irrelevant as carnal passion or erotic fantasy. The Viscount and Viscountess had a duty to their families and to their countries to produce a child or two and thus ensure the continuity of the title. That achieved, passion subsided and Gerald's sex-life became merely a series of fading memories.

Now, finding himself between the sheets with a sexy, exuberant woman, he was at a loss on how to behave. But it didn't matter. Semiramide had enthusiasm and experience enough for the two of them. She nibbled his ear: he found it tickled but also titillated. Gerald had a vague notion that he ought to be doing something with his own mouth. When an erect nipple was pushed between his lips, he reacted instinctively.

As his sexual excitement increased, a newly discovered energy took possession of his limbs. Almost without realizing it, he began to caress and fondle the fulsome curves of inviting womanhood which had so unexpectedly come into his life. However, the credit for passing from passionate petting to more serious business must be given to Semiramide. Having stroked Gerald's penis until it swelled up to a rich tumescence, she applied this organ to her lips. Gerald gave a tiny shudder, as he felt her tongue teasing him to an unimaginable vortex of pleasure. Then, Semiramide moved over his recumbent body and finally inserted his striving penis into her ripe, juicy vagina. Her hands clutched his shoulders as she forced herself down upon him and he strained to penetrate deeper inside her.

It did not last long. Gerald gasped and writhed as Semiramide's hot, wet pussy seemed to suck the sperm from the very depths of his body and out through his wildly ejaculating cock. As Lucinda was later to comment, it was not the fuck of the century, but, for Gerald, it was an experience of shattering novelty. Semiramide held him tight until his body had relaxed. Then, she tenderly, but dextrously, extricated his rapidly shrivelling member and snuggled up beside him with a contented sigh.

'Oh, Gerald,' she cooed, with hardly a hint of reproach in her voice. 'You seduced me.'

'I did?' Gerald was incredulous but knew better than to argue. 'By Jove, yes, I did.'

He was on the point of proferring an apology when Semiramide leaned over and kissed him.

'We must do it again,' she chuckled.

They did. Several times. And, strangely enough, the warmer waxed Gerald's affair with Semiramide, the more cordial became his relations with Hiram T. Watergate.

Indeed, such was the brimming goodwill of Hiram that, one evening after one of the now customary dinners at Hamblewood, he ventured to propose that Gerald might care to benefit from Hiram's fantastic talent for making money.

'Of course, if you feel that matters of commerce are too vulgar for anyone in your station of life, I would fully understand.'

'No, not at all, my dear fellow,' Gerald hastened to reassure Hiram. 'I think that I can claim to be as democratic as the next chap. I am not in the least snobbish – at least, as far as money is concerned.'

Consequently, when the party from 'Lucifer' arrived in Hamblewood, a few days later, they found the Viscount in high spirits. Lucinda was used to her father's fits of enthusiasm and his preoccupation with whatever was on his mind at any time, but, even so, she was rather taken aback by his lack of concern when she recounted their adventures on Xanthos.

'Don't you understand,' she mouthed her words slowly and deliberately, as if she were lecturing a retarded and inattentive child, 'we might have been killed!'

'Deuced disagreeable,' her parent assented airily.

Miles regarded his father thoughtfully. He sensed that the Viscount was nursing a secret and that he was bursting to tell them whatever it was that he had achieved and to revel in their admiration.

'You are in a good humour,' Miles accused.

'Of course he is. Mother's away,' Lucinda rejoined.

'No, it's something more than that.' Miles was in his legal mood. 'Own up, you have been up to something, haven't you.'

'You could say that,' Gerald purred. 'I have not been wasting my time while all the rest of the family has been cruising all over the world. As a matter of fact, I have just pulled off a business deal which will astound you.'

'Oh dear.' Lucinda was worried. 'I do hope that you have not done something stupid.'

'Not at all.' Gerald's cheeks flushed with indignation. 'Let me assure you that I have been able to enter into an association with one of the most astute men I have ever met in all my life.'

'Astute. Does that mean dishonest?' Sarah asked ingenuously.

'Good heavens, no! Hiram T. Watergate is an old friend: I trust him implicitly.'

'Hiram T. Watergate? I've never heard you mention him before. Just how old is this friendship?'

'You must appreciate, Miles,' Gerald replied defensively, 'it is not something that goes back far in time but it matured quickly. I feel as if I have known Hiram for years.'

'I think that you had better tell us about this deal from the beginning,' Miles said sternly but patiently.

'I shall, if you will only stop making such dashed stupid interruptions. To start with, do you realize that we have assets lying idle which could be earning us a lot of money?'

The Viscount glared around him as if to challenge anybody to contradict him.

'Such as what?' asked Miles.

'There's Hamblewood for example.'

'But you already charge people for visits,' Lucinda reminded him.

'That's what Hiram calls peanuts and pretzel money.'

'So what are you going to do to our house? Turn it into a brothel?'

'Really, Lucinda, how could you think of anything so coarse!' Her father was indignant, but with an effort, he controlled his emotions and he explained triumphantly to them, 'I'm prepared – in fact, I have already agreed to let a few of Hiram's friends stay here. Of course, they will pay for the privilege.'

'And how much have you agreed to give Hiram from what you take from your paying guests?'

'Not a penny. Miles. See what I mean about a great deal? He sends over the people and I collect.'

'And your new, old friend, Hiram, is prepared to go to all this trouble for nothing?' Lucinda's tone was sceptical.

'That's right. He will take his money out of what my friends pay when I send them out to stay at the Contessa's place.'

'Who is this Contessa? Another old buddy?'

'The Contessa de Scarpio is a very – er interesting and – er accomplished lady,' Lucinda's father answered her with some hesitancy.

Miles and Lucinda stared hard at him and Gerald averted his eyes, like a small boy who had been caught in the pantry.

'And the people who stay at Hamblewood will be personally selected from among her acquaintances by Semiramide – I mean the Contessa,' Gerald added.

'Semiramide? She sounds like a fancy pudding,' Miles commented.

'More likely, a tart,' Lucinda amended.

'Not at all, she is a charming woman. And she has a splendid place on the Adriatic – a veritable palace.'

'How do you know, father, dear? Have you seen it?'

'Not exactly, Lucinda. But I have a picture. Here, let me show you.'

The Viscount scurried away from his persecutors and returned, proudly bearing a multi-coloured postcard.

The picture on the card was of a stately, white building, standing in exotic gardens. The name of the establishment was printed on the back of the card and there was an inscription on the front. However, as both were in Cyrillic script, it needed a Russian scholar to decipher them. The exhibit was carefully scrutinized. Then, Brian who had remained silent throughout the proceedings, turned to Gerald who was posing as the vindicated viscount.

'Excuse me, Viscount Hamblewood, but may I ask if the Contessa actually claimed that this was a picture of her home?'

'Well, not in so many words. She apologized that she did not have a photograph of her place but said that this card would give me some idea of it.'

'She did not say anything more about it?'

'What more is there to say?' Gerald was becoming irritated by the lack of enthusiasm with which his business acumen was being greeted by the younger generation.

'When I was at school,' Brian continued, 'we had a headmaster who was mad keen on modern languages. I didn't learn French but I did study German and Russian for a couple of years. I'm no expert, but I do remember enough to be able to read and to translate what is written on that card.'

'Well?'

'That imposing building,' Brian stated deliberately, 'is the Lenin Institute for the Mentally Disordered. And it is not on the Adriatic: it is in Tbilisi, in Soviet Georgia.'

There was a moment's silence.

'And, as for the inscription on the front of the card,' Brian concluded, 'that reads – Fraternal Greetings on the Sixty-Fifth Anniversary of the Glorious October Revolution!'

'Perhaps she meant that her villa was similar – architecturally or something,' Gerald ventured without much conviction. 'Anyway, I recall now where she said her house is.' He smiled hopefully at his interrogators. 'It's in Italy – a place called Spoleto.'

'But, Spoleto is in Jugoslavia,' Sarah informed him.

'Doesn't sound Jugoslav,' Gerald objected.

'That's because its name was changed to Split years ago,' Miles said. 'And somehow, I don't think it likely that a Countess will own a stately home in socialist Jugoslavia, do you?'

'I'm sure that there is some simple explanation,' Gerald bleated.

'Let me ask you just one more question.' Miles' tone was quiet but tense. 'Did you, by any chance, put this cosy, little arrangement to take in each other's guests, in writing?'

27

'Now you come to mention it,' Gerald admitted, 'Hiram did scribble down something for me to sign.'

Lucinda groaned. Sarah rolled her eyes heaven-wards imploringly while Brian stared at the Viscount in evident disbelief.

'And do you have a copy of whatever it was that you signed?' Miles demanded.

'Of course I have. You don't think I'm stupid, do you?'

Miles refused to pass an opinion. 'May I see it, please?'

'I put it in my desk. Come into the study and I'll show you it.'

Silently, they all trooped after him into the study.

CHAPTER 3

It was quite late the following afternoon before Viscount Hamblewood located the missing scrap of paper which he had signed so casually. He produced it in triumph from among the jumble of unpaid bills, seed catalogues, invitations to open church fetes and begging letters, which constituted the Viscount's filing system, where it had been lurking.

'It's a sort of informal note – something to jog the memory, you know. Nothing official,' he explained.

Miles glanced at the document and gasped.

'Have you ever seen a chatty, little memorandum between a couple of pals which starts – "The first party to this agreement, Gerald Algernon St John Boscastle Farrer, Viscount Hamblewood and the Second Party, Hiram Thomas Washington Watergate do hereby agree and contract the following"?' he demanded.

'I never knew that his name was Washington,' mused his father. 'And I wonder who told him all my names.'

'It looks as if your friend did his homework before he unleashed his charm on you,' Miles answered.

'Or the charms of his phoney countess,' Lucinda added bitterly.

Gerald was stupefied. 'Do you really think that she could have been an imposter?' He shook his head like a bewildered sheep.

'Tell us the worst, Miles,' Lucinda said. 'What has our dear father got us into?'

Miles was silent. He concentrated on the paper and only replied when he had studied it closely for an eternity which lasted about ten minutes. His expression was grave.

'Of course, Hiram has another copy of this which you signed?' he asked his father.

Gerald nodded.

'You have committed yourself to an agreement which is remarkably precise and well drafted,' he told Gerald. 'I would say that it is legally binding. It has even been formally witnessed.'

'Yes, I remember now.' Gerald's eyes registered enlightenment. 'Hiram thought it would be a good idea if I got a couple of the servants to put their names on the paper. In case I lost it, you know, they would remember and be able to look for it without bothering me with going through all my papers. Come to think of it, I did consider it a bit odd, but I couldn't see that it could do any harm and after a couple of brandies, I must admit, it seemed rather a better idea than it does in the cold light of morning.'

Miles snorted. 'What you have promised this man is that he can send an unspecified number of guests of his choosing to Hamblewood in six months time and you will put them up and feed them for a weekly payment, which is described as a reasonable sum to be determined by Mr Watergate. He undertakes to find accommodation for your clients on similar terms the following year.'

'You mean it is only after we have taken in whoever Hiram cares to dump on us that we get a chance to hit back?'

'That's right, Lucinda.'

'And what happens if we object to Hiram's buddies?'

'That is quite clearly dealt with,' Miles informed them. 'In the event of non-fulfilment of the contract by either party, the agreement can be cancelled on payment of a penalty to compensate the other party.'

'How much?' asked Sarah.

'One million dollars,' Miles replied.

Four pairs of eyes gazed at Gerald in consternation. He blinked and shuffled from one foot to the other.

'It will probably be all right,' the peer pleaded. 'I don't think that we should jump to any conclusions until we hear what Hiram intends. I mean to say, he was so friendly, and the Contessa – '

'Ah, yes, the glamorous Contessa,' Lucinda breathed venomously. 'Every good mouse trap needs a tasty bit of cheese. Did she somehow find her way into your bed?'

The question took the Viscount by surprise.

'Good Heavens! Really, you have no right to suggest such a thing to your own father,' he protested.

Lucinda stared at him unflinchingly. He faltered.

'I don't know what your mother would say if she were here. We were just good friends. Very good friends,' he added.

Lucinda continued to pierce his guilty conscience with icy, blue eyes.

'It wasn't like that,' mumbled Gerald.

'Did she seduce you?' Lucinda hissed.

'Good Lord, no. She said that I seduced her,' the noble lord admitted. There could have been a faint trace of pride mingled with the shame of his confession.

'That's it, then,' Lucinda said hopelessly. 'You have been well and truly taken!'

Any lingering hope they may have entertained was extinguished when the afternoon post arrived. It included a letter from Hiram T. Watergate in which he requested that preparations should be put in hand for the eventual arrival of two hundred and forty 'patients'. There was no indication of what illness afflicted Gerald's future guests.

'And what do you think Mother will say when she returns from the States and finds the house crammed full of the walking dead?' Miles asked.

His father shuddered. The prospect was too dreadful to contemplate.

'You will just have to pay up,' Lucinda told him. 'That is, if the agreement is as water-tight as Miles says it is.'

'I'm sure of that,' her brother said.

'But I can't,' wailed the hapless Viscount.

'But we must have the money,' said Lucinda. 'I mean to say, look at all this.' She waved her hand to take in the sumptuous mansion and its treasures. 'Surely, we are very rich?'

'Of course we are rich,' Gerald retorted. 'But we don't keep a million dollars in the house-keeping account at the bank.'

'Well, you will simply have to sell some shares or something,' Lucinda snapped.

'But I can't. Everything is in Melánie's name. There is no way I can lay my hands on any big money without going to your mother. And how could I ask her for a million dollars without going into the reason? I dare not have Hiram's regiment here when Melanie gets back and there is no way I can pay him off. The thing is hopeless.'

'Don't say that,' Sarah attempted to comfort him. 'There must be something that we can do.'

'Of course there is,' Lucinda stated. 'I have the beginning of an idea already. But we shall need careful planning. And you,' she told her father accusingly, 'will have to do as you are told.'

The Viscount's silence was taken as acquiescence.

PART II

                      'Fie, for shame!
'Twill set a virgin's blood on flame.
This to fifteen a proper gift!
It might lend sixty-five a lift.
I know your maiden aunt will scold,
And think my present somewhat bold.
I see her lift her hands and eyes:
"What; eat it, niece; eat Spanish flies!"

(To a Young Lady with some Lampreys.)
                                  JOHN GAY

CHAPTER 4

Several days had elapsed and Viscount Hamblewood, in a puzzled frame of mind, was fastening his safety belt as the Air France jet came in to land at Nice. It seemed bizarre that at a time of crisis in which he was the central character he should have been despatched on some wild goose chase. Yet, Lucinda and her three companions had been insistent that he should rush off without delay to find Jennifer aboard 'Lucifer' and bring back some extraordinary herbal remedy which she had on the yacht. Lucinda had sworn that it was the only thing which would be an effective cure and it was only some hours after he had departed that the Viscount had realized that he was not aware that his daughter, or any of the others, was ill. Indeed, he might have suspected that they were up to some mischief and wanted him out of the way from the urgency with which they had practically thrust him out of his own house. When he had suggested that one of the others might undertake the errand, Miles had pleaded that he had to appear in court in London, Sarah had stated that her pregnancy had reached a delicate stage, Lucinda had felt ill and Brian was simply nowhere to be found. A man less trusting than Gerald Farrer, Viscount Hamblewood, might have sniffed a conspiracy, but as Hiram T. Watergate and Semiramide, Contessa de Scarpio, would confirm, he was possessed of a very trusting character.

In the days leading up to his journey, Gerald had endeavoured to think of some way of raising a million dollars without mortgaging Hamblewood and thus apprising his wife of his predicament. Reluctantly, he had come to the conclusion that putting a gigantic bet on a horse was far too hazardous and, anyway, where was he going to get the cash he would need as a stake? And the same went for plunging into the Stock Market. Viscount Hamblewood was baffled.

Not so his daughter. She had decided to take matters into her own hands after the arrival of a letter to Miles. He had made some enquiries in New York on the activities of Mr Watergate and the reply had not been encouraging. It seemed that the Viscount's business partner had flitted from one racket to the next and was currently running something called the Deare Center. Miles' informant stated that this was a sort of clinic cum rest home which provided over-priced psychiatric guidance for wealthy hypochondriacs. Sooner or later, the authorities would close the place down, but meanwhile, it soaked up money from the inmates as if its walls were made of blotting paper. There was also a rumour that the Deare Center had come to some arrangement with a similar lodging house for lunatics in rural England. So, now they knew why Hiram had put in his demand for two hundred and forty beds.

The four younger members of the household held a hastily convened council of war while Gerald was pottering around the gardens one morning. It was then that Lucinda proposed her plan of campaign.

'We have to raise this million dollars because it is obvious that father will not manage it himself. And we have less than six months. So, what is it that sells faster and surer than anything else?'

The others regarded her curiously.

'It's obvious isn't it?' Lucinda told them. 'Sex.'

'Sex?' Miles echoed incredulously. 'My God, Lucinda, even you couldn't entertain that number of men in so short a time.'

Lucinda glared at Miles with the concentrated scorn which sisters reserve for their brothers.

'Hiram T. Con-man said one true thing in his sales talk,' she said. 'This house is an asset which can be used to earn big money. Of course, we have visitors who pay to be ushered around and have pointed out to them the best of our pictures and furniture. But other houses do much better. Why? Because they have some gimmick – a safari park or a museum of ancient motor cars, that sort of thing. Now, why don't we use the biggest and best gimmick of all, sex? Think of it, we could let couples have ten minutes on the bed in which Queen Elizabeth I slept. All those kids who would be told that they were conceived in a royal bed! We could sell all sorts of interesting gadgets instead of a lot of boring souvenirs and we could certainly hot up the post-cards.'

'Do you really think that people would come?' asked Brian.

'I am sure they would if we used the right publicity. I would advertise "Hamblewood – the Heart of Britain. Come to the Love-in of the Lords."'

'How vulgar!' Miles objected.

'Lucinda's right,' Sarah countered. 'What we need is a lot of vulgar money.'

'It can't possibly fail,' Lucinda continued. 'You see, I propose that we smuggle in a consignment of our wonder heather which we took from Xanthos. A tiny dose of the heather liquor dispensed in the refreshments served in the cafeteria will work wonders. Anybody who comes to Hamblewood and has a cup of tea will experience the most thrilling and compelling sex of his or her life. Once the news begins to spread, we shall have more customers than we can manage.'

'Yes,' Brian reflected. 'And this nectar which we distil is not even a recognized drug, so we shan't have any problems with the narcotics squads. Once Hamblewood has a reputation as the country's sex centre, we could even market some of the nectar preparations nationally.'

'I thought of that,' Lucinda added eagerly. 'We could launch the first chain of sex-supermarkets.'

'What about your father?' Sarah asked.

'We'll have to get him out of the way while we get the thing going. Once we are in full production, and the turnstiles are clicking merrily, he will accept the situation. After all, it's his fault that we are having to go commercial, isn't it?'

'I am sure that he will be happier with the supermarkets than with the use of his house as a bordello,' Miles remarked. 'It's not what is expected of a viscount.'

'That will be a great brand name for the goods we sell in the supermarkets,' Lucinda enthused. 'Can't you visualize the notices "Straight from Hamblewood – Today's special offer – The Vice-Count Vibrator". And we could use a coronet as a trade-mark.'

'Put a coronet on your cunt,' Brian chuckled.

'I'm not sure that I like the idea,' Miles commented. 'But there does not seem to be any other way of raising the sort of money that we need.'

'Right, that's settled, then.' Lucinda was at her briskest and bossiest. 'Now, we have to get Father out of circulation while we get things moving.'

'Couldn't you persuade him to go to France and pick up the heather which we shall need?' Brian suggested.

And that is how it came about that a few days later,

Gerald was fumbling with his safety belt as the plane descended towards Nice.

CHAPTER 5

It was good to be back in England, or so thought Viscount Hamblewood, as he settled back in the Rolls Royce which had met him at the airport. Not that he had suffered unduly in France. He had eaten well, the wine was excellent, the sun still shone on the Riviera and Jennifer had made him more than welcome. Yet, he never felt completely at ease when he was abroad. There was something about other countries which Viscount Hamblewood decided was foreign. Now, he was back, passing through familiar landscapes, among his own people and he was happy in that sense of security which came from being back in his own element. The great thing about England, he concluded, was that it never changed: you could depend on everything being just as it used to be.

But, in this Viscount Hamblewood was mistaken. As the dignified black saloon drove slowly through the lodge gates, there was an unusual and rather unwelcome sense of bustle and activity about the place.

'What are all those damned cars doing here?' Viscount Hamblewood asked.

'I have no idea, my lord,' replied the chauffeur.

There were certainly more people about than should have been the case since he had got back early, before the customary hour at which the great house was opened to the public. A lot of them were carrying cameras, something which was not permitted inside, and some even had tape recorders.

'Who are all these?' Viscount Hamblewood asked Sarah, who was standing at the door to greet him, as he emerged from the car and waved uncertainly at the invading throng.

'Oh, that's just the press.' Sarah dismissed the matter. 'Have you got the plants?'

'Yes, of course. I'll let Lucinda have them when I have finished unpacking.'

'No, no, now, please!' Sarah demanded.

Gerald could see no reason for this unseemly haste, but he had no wish to upset Sarah. He had a notion that pregnant women were subject to irrational whims that had to be obeyed or they would dissolve into a fit of hysterics and probably suffer a miscarriage. So, he rummaged about until he found the large Dior hat-box which he handed to Sarah who grabbed it and ran off into the house without another word.

Deuced odd, thought Gerald, as he followed in a more leisurely fashion. He went upstairs, had a shower and changed into some more comfortable clothes. It was nearly an hour after his arrival when Gerald made his way downstairs and approached the main dining hall. His way was barred by Thistlethwaite, the butler.

'Welcome back, my lord, Miss Lucinda requested me to suggest that you adjourn to the library.'

'What the devil is going on? Can't I walk into my own hall?' Gerald bristled with indignation.

'It might be inadvisable, my lord. Miss Lucinda is conducting a press conference there.'

'Oh, my God!' Gerald fled to the fastness of the library.

Meanwhile, in the great hall, Lucinda was doing her best to win the support of the ladies and gentlemen of the press for the Sex Centre of England, Hamblewood, the stately home with a heart (and other relevant organs).

It was not easy. She spoke of the permissive society but her audience were showing signs of restiveness. They had heard it all before. A few reporters were interested.

'Will there be bestiality?' asked the man from *Pravda*, a heavily built, shaggy man with bushy eyebrows and an even bushier beard.

'You'll have to bring your own bear,' Lucinda informed him.

'Let me get this quite straight.' The *Newsweek* reporter was a wiry, nervous man with glasses. 'Are you claiming that Hamblewood will become for sex what Las Vegas is for gambling?'

'Better than that. Here, there will be no losers, as you will see in a little while.'

'It could never have happened under Franco,' muttered the representative of *El Pais*.

A formidable looking woman, dressed in sober tweeds got to her feet. She transfixed Lucinda with a gimlet eye.

'Young woman, I am from the Lord's Day Observance Society. I regard the whole project as disgusting. However, I presume that you retain a spark of decency and will ensure that this House of Evil will remain closed on the sabbath day.'

'Not at all,' rejoined Lucinda. 'We expect bigger crowds than ever on Sundays when we shall provide every facility for people to obey the biblical commandment – "Love thy Neighbour!" Instead of hearing about it in church, here they can practice what you preach.'

There was a faint patter of applause but it was evident to Lucinda that most of the reporters remained sceptical. One, at least, was downright hostile.

'Do you frigid English believe that you can set up this old country house as a rival to Paris?' The man from *Figaro* was furious at the effrontery of the sexless Anglo-Saxons.

Miles decided that this was a situation requiring the finesse of a lawyer.

'I would remind you,' he stated in an authoritative tone, 'that the treaty setting up the Common Market insisted on there being fair competition within the European Community.'

'Ridiculous!' jeered *Figaro*. 'Who would want to come and make love in your house in preference to Pigalle?'

'Or the Reeperbahn in Hamburg,' added *Der Spiegel*.

'Or by the Amsterdam canals,' said *De Telegraaf*.

A gentleman from New Orleans was on the point of giving a verbal tour of Basin Street, when Sarah slipped into the room and nodded to Lucinda.

'Thank God!' Lucinda breathed. 'Just in time.'

There was an astonished silence as Thistlethwaite came into the hall, pushing an elegant trolley on which were placed cups and saucers and a large urn of hot tea. Lucinda took advantage of the respite to reassert her authority.

'We are inviting you to inspect the rooms which will shortly be open to the public. But, first, we would like you to sample the refreshments which will be available.'

'Tea!' scoffed *Figaro*. 'When a Frenchman would make passionate love, the English drink tea.'

'This is rather special tea,' said Lucinda. 'Do try it and let me know how you like it.'

'Haven't you got anything stronger?' demanded *Christian Science Monitor*.

'Have a cup of this brew first. Then tell us if you find it too weak,' Miles advised.

While the press were disconsolately sipping their tea, the man from *The Times* addressed Lucinda.

'I have heard a rumour that you invited a member of the royal family to formally open the centre, Miss Farrer. Is there any truth in it?'

'We did consider asking Prince Andrew but we were informed that he would be away on a state visit to some island in the Caribbean,' Lucinda replied. 'However, we have been lucky enough to get Xaviera Hollander to deputize for him. She should be arriving this afternoon, so if you stay on, you will have the chance to meet her.'

This announcement was greeted with considerably more enthusiasm than that which had been accorded to the tea. However, as the assembled news-hounds drank, there was a perceptible change in the atmosphere. The guy from *Penthouse* was positively leering at the gal from *Playboy* and *Church Times* was giggling as if he had heard a dirty joke for the first time in his life. The *New Statesman* seemed to be attempting to remove a stain from the inside of *La Prensa*'s blouse while the uninhibited representative of the *Journal de Genève* was unashamedly masturbating.

'If you would like to look around,' Lucinda proposed, 'everything should be ready for you.'

There was a mad rush in the direction of the bedrooms.

Gerald, having taken refuge in the library, heard the stampede and decided that it would be safer to remain secluded in his lair.

Meanwhile, strange happenings were taking place in the various rooms and apartments of the noble house, where the ladies and gentlemen of the press were inspecting and trying out the amenities. In one majestic bed, *Figaro* had apparently forgotten about the charms of Pigalle and he had found something better to do with his tongue than talking. With him, under the canopy of the four poster bed, *Spiegel*, *News of the World* and *Times of India* had formed a colourful daisy-chain. In an adjoining room, there had been a sensational fusion of *Playboy* and *Penthouse* beneath a vast Rubens painting of the Rape of the Sabine Women.

Downstairs, several of the original dungeons had been transformed into torture chambers and inside one of them, a strange ritual was in progress. The burly, hairy *Pravda* was suspended by his manacled wrists from an oak beam, a sackcloth hood over his head, iron chains around his ankles and weights hanging from his testicles. Behind him stood the Lord's Day Observance Society. Her severe tweed suit had been discarded and she had shaken her hair free. It streamed behind her like a fantastic mane, as she lashed the moaning Russian with a vicious rawhide whip. For the occasion, she had put on some clothes which had been thoughtfully left in the dungeon for use by the customers. It was probably the first time in her life that she had ever worn black leather and there was something about the way it clung to her thighs and her breasts which was giving her a new slant on life. Her eyes glittered as she twitched the whip over the buttocks of the squirming *Pravda*, flicking her wrist to make sure that the tip of the whip would curl around and cut into her victim's balls. Between each stroke, she called him names which could never have previously passed her lips – and certainly never on Sundays! The suspended Slav screamed with pain and pleasure at every lash.

A more tender encounter was taking place in a tiny room at the top of a turret, the sort of place where, in some fairy tale, a beautiful princess would have been imprisoned until she was rescued by a Prince Charming or the youngest son of a youngest son.

For several months before the Hamblewood Happening, the young cub reporter from *New Society* had been casting longing gazes at the pretty girl who covered social events for the *Guardian*. But he was far too timid to approach her. After all, he was only a beginner in the profession whereas she was established – on the permanent staff with her own desk and typewriter – as much above his station in life as the princess was above the youngest son of a youngest son. From time to time, they had covered the same assignments and just once, he had plucked up the courage to invite her to join him for a cup of coffee but before he could speak, she had been carried off by the great, strapping Adonis from the *Daily Express*.

When Thistlethwaite came to dispense the magic tea, *New Society* had managed to find himself a seat next to the goddess from the *Guardian*. He had smiled at her and attempted to say what a lovely day it was, but the words had died in his throat. She was impossibly beautiful and he was catastrophically shy. Still, she had smiled back before getting absorbed in a conversation with the far from shy *Daily Express*.

Then, came the tea. It tasted a little odd but quite pleasant and *New Society* felt a soft glow, not only in his stomach, but in more unexpected parts of his anatomy. He looked at the *Guardian* and there was something in the way she looked back at him which spoke to him clearer and louder than any words. As if by some pre-arranged signal, they got to their feet and walked slowly out of the hall. Without realizing it, he took her hand. It was warm and soft and he squeezed it gently. To his amazement, she returned the pressure and moved closer to him as they mounted the staircase. They had only the vaguest idea of the geography of the house and they wandered from one floor to the next, but when they reached the intimacy of the turret room, they knew that this place was for them.

New Society closed the door behind them and took the princess in his arms. Her face was tilted up to meet his lips and in the thrill of that first kiss, *New Society* drank in all the sweetness that he had dreamed of all his life. He went to speak, but she silenced him with a finger on his mouth.

It was as if she could read his most secret thoughts. She unbuttoned his shirt and ran her fingers through the fine hair on his chest. Suddenly his shyness was a thing of the past. He held her in his arms as surely and masterfully as if he were the man from the *Express*. His own hands were inside her blouse. He felt the fine lines of her shoulders, the melting softness of her skin and her living warmth beneath his hands as he gloried in the swelling of her breasts, delicate yet firm, with her nipples rising taut beneath his adoring fingers.

As if in some silent movie, they went over to the bed. He laid her tenderly on the soft, pink bed-cover and swiftly removed his clothes. She had kicked off her shoes and peeled off her tights. Her skirt and blouse were dropped onto the floor and she wore only a wisp of nylon as panties, as she regarded him in his nakedness.

He was about to join her on the bed but first she took his straining penis in her hand with infinite gentleness, stroked it and then placed it lovingly in her mouth. He felt the sweet embrace of her lips: the pleasure was almost unendurable. She licked him with a lascivious slowness which sent shivers down his spine and made him ache to penetrate her.

Again, as if by the same miraculous telepathy, she responded. Releasing him, she pulled off her panties, the last veil. Gratefully, he buried his head in the silk of her chestnut pubic hairs. He worshipped at her Mound of Venus like some overawed pilgrim and kissed, licked and nuzzled the beckoning lips of her salt-sweet vagina. She caressed his head and then motioned him to arise. As he moved over her body, he paused to pay homage with his lips to her supple stomach, the tiny goblet of her navel and the fragrance of her breasts. Then, she deftly guided his rigid penis into her and he was engulfed by her satiny smoothness.

Nobody had ever made love as they made love. The earth stood still: time ceased to exist. His hands roamed over her body while she clasped him tight, as if to bind him to her for ever. They moved rhythmically, perfectly at one, slowly, sinuously and totally absorbed with each other. Every sensation was a wonder.

'Oh, my darling, you cannot know how much I have wanted you,' he told her, his voice husky with emotion.

She kissed him hungrily, her tongue thrusting into his mouth. Her breath was sweet; his head was spinning with excitement. If only this moment could last for all eternity.

But it couldn't. Their movements were becoming more agitated as their passion mounted. He was gasping and her breathing was quick and shallow and she was making short, broken noises, her hands clutching him, her legs intertwined around his, forcing him deeper and deeper within her, possessing him. The gentleness disappeared from their mating; they were absolutely in the power of an animal emotion. She could sense that he was near his climax. His balls were tight and the relentless piston of his penis was as hard as steel. Her own juices were overflowing, soaking him as she sucked him further in, greedily claiming him as her own. She felt that strange near numbness as her muscles took on a life of their own. Neither of them had any more control over their own bodies: it was as though they had become merely extensions of their own sexualities. They were swept up in one great onrush and their bodies rocked and shuddered as they burst into a frenzied orgasm. Her cunt was quivering wildly as he spurted his hot sperm, again and again into her.

It was some time before they were sufficiently recovered to make a move. *New Society* gazed up at the *Guardian* in hope, mingled with doubt. Was it all over, a single, unaccountable episode in their lives and would she be as remote as ever tomorrow? She understood the unasked question. Taking his hand in hers, she kissed him again, lightly but reassuringly. Only then did he dare to ask,

'My sweet, what is your name?'

Viscount Hamblewood was tired of being confined to the library. He had a vague idea that tea should have been served but decided to give it a miss since it appeared to have given him a miss. He strolled over to where the port decanter should have been standing but it was not there. Probably been taken by Thistlethwaite either for refilling or for him to take a sly drink, mused Gerald. He presumed that the butler did indulge in an occasional tipple and his lordship came to the decision to inspect what was available downstairs in the wine cellars.

Having descended, he was conscious of a strange moaning from nearby. It was the sort of noise which ought to be investigated. He opened the door from behind which the sound had come and was unable to believe the evidence of his eyes. A naked, hairy man was hanging from a post with chains all over his body and a female fury, clad in black leather and brandishing a fearsome whip was standing before him, hissing curses and insults at him.

'Good Heavens, madam, have you taken leave of your senses?' enquired the dumbfounded Viscount.

'Who asked you to interfere? Get out!' roared *Pravda*.

Baffled, Gerald withdrew.

CHAPTER 6

'If you go to football this Saturday, I want a day out on Sunday.'

'You can do as you like. It's my day off and I'm going to take it easy.'

Mary Reynolds was not surprised by her husband's reply. She was a pleasant looking woman, fair with a fresh complexion, short and small boned so that she resembled an oversized doll. Mary was twenty-five and had been married for three years but she and Tommy had as yet no children. Tommy worked in a garage and Mary was a cashier at a local supermarket. Life had been fun when they started going out together and for the first couple of years of their marriage, but it had now settled down into a routine. Every day, Tommy would bring Mary a cup of tea in bed. Then, by the time he had washed and shaved, she would have prepared breakfast. Tommy would drive to work: Mary's supermarket was nearby, so she walked. They each had a snack at lunch time and Mary would cook an evening meal which would be ready by the time that Tommy got home. Together, they would wash up and clear away after their dinner before watching television, exchanging gossip and finally going to bed. The only break in this constant pattern came at the weekend. But Tommy was a football fanatic, whereas Mary could not tell a centre·half from a goal-post and could not have cared less. If United were playing at home, Tommy would be there, on the terrace, cheering on his side, even if Mary were at death's doorstep. On Saturdays, Mary would go shopping, do odd jobs in the house and sometimes spend a little time with her mother or her friends, but there were days when she got a bit fed up with Tommy's obsession. The trouble was that after his outing on Saturday, Tommy rarely felt like going out on Sunday, which was when Mary wanted to get away from the home and the house work for a while.

She felt that she needed a break and, glancing through the newspaper, she had seen something about Hamblewood.

'Listen, Tommy. This Hamblewood sounds ever so romantic. Let's have an early dinner on Sunday and go and see what it's like.'

But Tommy was unsympathetic. 'A lot of bloody nonsense, I'll be bound,' he scoffed. 'If it's a nice day, there's plenty that needs doing in the garden.'

Usually, Mary gave way, but this time, she was determined to have her day out. So, that Sunday she got up early, roasted a leg of pork and vegetables and made a pudding for dessert. Her brother, Alex, had come around and the three of them ate together. Then, as the men started to clear the table, she went upstairs, changed into a summery frock and put on her coat.

'Where are you off to?' Tommy called, as she came down the staircase.

'I told you yesterday. I am going to this Hamblewood place. If you want to come along – '

'No,' Tommy dismissed her invitation with a toss of his head. 'I'll stay home. Perhaps Alex will give me a hand in the garden.'

'Who are you kidding? Once the pair of you have settled in the armchairs, an atomic bomb wouldn't shift you, I'm taking the car.'

'Enjoy yourself. When will you be back?'

'I don't know. It depends on how I like it.'

And with those words, Mary Reynolds, shut the street door behind her and set off on an adventure.

It was the middle of the afternoon when she drove through the imposing gateway and found her way to the visitors car park.

'I hope I'm not too late,' she said to the nice young man who was taking money for admission in the entrance lobby of the house.

'No, you'll find that there is always something going on in Hamblewood,' smiled Brian. 'If you are on your own, you might like to join a guided tour. You'll find a group, leaving from the Dining Hall.'

Mary decided to follow Brian's advice. With the rest of a party, she found herself led into the Nell Gwynn Room. In this very chamber, she learned, Charles II, 'The Merry Monarch' had his way with Mistress Gwynn. Then, the resourceful orange seller had her way with the king. To remove any doubts on the subject, a short, specially made film was shown which taught Mary a lot about Restoration England which she had never heard about at school. However, the exhibit which made the greatest impression on her was the Long Gallery, where a live show was being staged. It was called Passion of the Pasha. The Gallery had been transformed into part of the seraglio and there must have been at least a score of nubile, young women, enticingly dressed in harem pants and tiny tunics which enhanced the sensuality of the odalisques. A fragrant, spicy aroma hung heavily in the room and there was a subdued lilt of oriental music in the background. Very much in the foreground was a splendidly built 'Pasha', sprawling on a divan, who was entertaining himself with a couple of the loveliest women that Mary had ever seen. She gazed, open mouthed, at the decadent dalliance which was taking place. This was certainly more fascinating than a football match and she had to admit that the Pasha was a more magnificent specimen than her Tommy.

There were a number of other erotic exhibits and some of more general interest. After they had stood reverently before the very bed in which Queen Bess had shown favour to Essex, the guide addressed his flock.

'That is the end of what might be called the historical tour of the house. Now, we come to something rather different and the most popular part with most of our visitors. However, before we continue, you are all invited to take a little refreshment with the compliments of the Farrer family, your hosts.'

Nobody refused the free drink and the biscuits which were served. There was a strange alcoholic brew and some coffee: Mary, conscious of the fact that she was going to drive home, restricted herself to a cup of coffee. At any rate she thought, that can't do any harm.

After that, everything seemed to be changed – the house, the guides and the men and women who were strolling around. Mary felt that she was seeking somebody, a man or woman who was waiting for her.

And then she saw Helena. She was a tall woman with delicate, coffee coloured skin, probably from one of the islands in the Caribbean. She was wearing skin tight pants which emphasized the beauty of her slender legs. There was a quality in the way she looked at Mary which both beckoned and commanded her. Mary was aware of a quickening of her senses, a consciousness of her own body and a feeling of being more alive than she had ever experienced before. She felt herself irresistibly attracted by this unknown woman. More than anything else in the world, she wanted to make love to her.

Hamblewood had become a fairy palace of sensuality. Discreet notices indicated the way to such spots as Lounge for Leather-Lovers, The Gay Gallery, Kinky Korner, Torture Dungeons, First Floor for Fetishists and, inevitably, The Sex Souvenir Shop. Helena took her hand and they walked the length of a corridor, glancing into several rooms. Many of them were sparsely furnished with either a bed or a mattress on the floor, often occupied by other amorous sightseers. Mary glimpsed a wild orgy taking place on a group of mattresses, but her companion led her into a smaller, still unoccupied, room.

'Have you ever made love to a woman?' she asked.

Mary shook her head. She felt weak with desire. She wanted this woman to take her in sweetness and love.

'My name is Helena. And you are?'

'Mary.'

'Well, Mary, this is an afternoon that I know we shall both remember all our lives.'

Helena drew Mary close and kissed her. Mary thrilled to the unfamiliar scent, the caress of Helena's hands and the tenderness which seemed to radiate from the woman. With light fingers, Helena undressed Mary and then looked longingly at her body, exposed and vulnerable. She slipped out of her own clothes and Mary was possessed by an overwhelming lust for the dark skinned, masterful woman who led her towards an ornate Regency bed.

They embraced, their limbs intertwined as if to fuse together their burning bodies. Helena's sensuous fingers explored every inch of her body and Mary's flesh glowed beneath her lover's touch. For the first time in her life, she realized the sexual potency of her toes, her ears, the nape of her neck, the ripe swelling of her thighs.

'That's what men don't realize,' whispered Helena, as she burrowed her delicate nose under Mary's armpit and licked the tangy, golden hairs. 'A woman needs to have love made to the whole of her body, not just her pussy.'

Mary stroked her partner's tight, black curls and let her hands fall onto her polished shoulders. She marvelled at the subtle blending of softness and strength in those supple limbs. Then her lips paid adoring tribute to Helena's firm breasts and the dark mauve rosebuds of her nipples. Her hand groped between those superb legs and she felt the dewy dampness of the lips of Helena's vagina and her mouth watered at the prospect of tasting those love juices.

They twisted and turned. At times they were feverishly seeking each other, thrusting fingers and tongues and shaking with excitement. Then, as one bombshell of an orgasm after another died, there were spells of such gentle tenderness that Mary felt tears of happiness welling up in her eyes. Helena murmured words of endearment into her ear and Mary kissed her gratefully for the new life which Helena had brought to her.

However, everything eventually has to come to an end and reluctantly the couple put on their clothes and wandered, hand in hand, back to the lobby.

'Shall I see you again?' Mary asked.

Helena shook her head with a sad smile. 'No, what we have had together was perfect, let's not spoil it. If we go on meeting, you will want to know more about me and familiarity kills romance. But when you make love to some other woman, or maybe with some man, you will remember me and our afternoon and that will add a little magic to your love-making. And that, dearest Mary, will be Helena's present to you, a gift that will last as long as you experience love.'

She pressed a final kiss on Mary's lips, turned away, and walked briskly through the crowd and out of Mary's life, retaining to the end a sense of mystery. Mary might have followed her, but, instinctively, she knew that it would have been a mistake and that Helena had been right in leaving her with a memory which would never grow stale. With a sigh, she turned back to the display of souvenirs on sale to see if there was anything that might prove an inspiration for Tommy. Unfortunately, there was not a codpiece in United's colours.

Back home, she found Alex and Tommy still hard at work at their armchair gardening.

'Give us a cup of tea, love, I'm parched,' called the man in her life, as she came through the door.

'Did you have a good time?' her brother asked.

'Yes, lovely,' Mary answered dreamily. 'But, you know there is so much to see there, I think I shall go again. But it's not a place for you, dear,' she said to Tommy. 'I'll probably go on a Saturday when you are at football.'

'Good idea,' assented Tommy. 'It will give you an interest and something to look forward to.'

'That's right,' she said.

Mary went into the kitchen so Tommy never saw the broad smile which spread across her face or the sparkle in her eyes.

CHAPTER 7

The turnstiles whirled round giddily and lucratively throughout the summer, at least on the sunny days. At the same time, Lucinda and Miles worked like fiends to get the first of the Sex Supermarkets into operation. Their ventures attracted a considerable amount of publicity which helped to bring in the customers. The fact that a lot of the comment was critical made no difference. Every time that they were denounced from press or pulpit, sales soared.

However, they were never able to forget that they were working against the calendar: they had to meet their deadline or all their efforts would have been in vain. Sarah was appointed unofficial treasurer and they met frequently to review their progress.

One of these meetings was in session. It was a drizzly Monday morning, the sort of day that would depress the most sanguine and drive a Samaritan to drink or suicide. It was too early for the house to be open to the public, not that many were likely to turn up.

The mood of the meeting matched the weather. There was an underlying feeling of gloom and doom, despite an optimistic report by Lucinda on some recent developments.

'We have started selling a couple of sexually stimulating drinks in the supermarkets,' she announced. 'Of course, they are based on the same distilled heather which we dispense in Hamblewood and as they contain no recognized drug, they have been cleared by the Home Office, or whoever it is who is responsible for protecting the public from being more seriously poisoned than is customary in restaurants.'

She paused and regarded the faces of her listeners. There was not a glimmer of a smile, so, with a faint sigh, she resumed.

'The stuff you brew in a pot, we have marketed under the name of "Ero-Tea". The other more exotic tipple is hotted up by the addition of a generous ration of rum and fruit juices and its effects are sensational. We sell it as "Stiff Cock-tail".

'We did come up against one minor unexpected problem. You recall that we have started selling "Vice-Count"

Vibrators. Well, one obscure and extreme feminist group objected. They claimed that the name was sexist and demanded that we change it to "Vice-Countess".'

'What have you done?' asked her bewildered parent.

'Changed it to "Vice-Cunt",' Lucinda replied.

Before the Viscount had a chance to vent his displeasure, Lucinda turned to Brian and asked, 'What have you been doing at Hamblewood while I've been away, working on the supermarkets?'

'Well, you might have noticed that we have made a few alterations in the yew alley.'

'The yew alley!' gasped Gerald. 'Young man, do you realize that those yews have grown there for three centuries, the moss floor is like velvet. Why, the place is a jewel, one of the treasures of England.' Words failed him and he sat, opening and closing his mouth in silence, like a goldfish who had just learned the terrible facts of life about pussy cats.

'Oh, we haven't interfered with the place structurally,' Brian reassured him. 'It's simply what you might call the presentation that's been modified. We call it "The Meat Rack" and we charge unaccompanied visitors for admission.'

'And what do they do there?' Gerald was not mollified.

'They just walk up and down and look at each other,' Brian told him.

'What on earth for?'

'Don't you know,' Lucinda interrupted, 'that in a big store, The Meat Rack is where you can have a look at what meat is on offer?'

'You mean that our yew alley is used as a place for dubious assignations?' Gerald's voice quivered with emotion.

'That's right,' Sarah said, 'but don't let it worry you. It really is paying off very well.'

'I'm afraid that this is not getting us anywhere,' Miles said emphatically. 'We have to face facts. Do you realize that we now have less than two months to go before we will be obliged to pay off your Hiram T. Watergate or take the consequences? Everybody has worked his or her ass off, setting up Meat Racks, Mistresses on the Mattresses, The Rubber Refectory, Sodomites in the Cellar and all the rest. But just look at the figures of what we have taken. We are making money, but nowhere near fast enough to meet our deadline. The truth is that there is no way that Hamblewood and the Supermarkets can possibly raise sufficient cash in time.'

They all knew that Miles was right but nobody had wanted to admit it.

Their deliberations were interrupted by the arrival of Thistlethwaite.

The butler coughed nervously. 'Excuse me, Miss Lucinda, but there is a gentleman asking to see you.'

'Show him into the library. I'll be with him when we have finished here. It's probably somebody who manufactures some gadget which he wants us to market or another damned journalist,' Lucinda commented irritably.

'I am afraid that is not the case.' Thistlethwaite was plainly embarrassed. 'The gentleman claims to be a member of your family and insists that his business with you is of the greatest urgency.'

'Who the devil can it be?' queried Miles. 'Anyway, he will have to wait.'

'Now that is hardly what I would call a warm welcome to your favourite uncle who has come half way across the world to see you.'

The speaker was a man in his middle fifties who had

quietly followed the butler into the room. His grey hair and beard were neatly trimmed and there was an impish sense of fun in the way he regarded them with his alert, blue eyes.

The four of them gazed in astonishment at Ulysses Blake, lately Lord of Xanthos and their implacable enemy.

'How the hell did you get here?'

'Really, Lucinda, what a greeting! No fond kiss? If I did not know what a sweet loving girl you are, I would have got the impression that you weren't glad to see me.'

'Why aren't you tucked up comfortably in one of the world's less luxurious prisons?' asked Brian.

'You all disappoint me. I have come here because you need my help and I am prepared to give it.'

Miles snorted in disbelief and derision but before he could answer, Ulysses continued,

'Now, don't say something which you will regret.' His tone was one of sweet reasonableness but there was an undertone of amusement which he could not completely suppress. 'I know that when we last met, we had our differences and I would be less than honest if I didn't admit that I was pretty sore at you for ruining a honey of a racket which I had going. But that's over and done with. I assure you that I have not the least resentment and I am absolutely sincere in my offer of help.'

'What makes you think that we could ever trust you?'

'My dear Lucinda, I couldn't get you into a worse mess than you are in already. Let's face it. In crude terms you owe one long one and you haven't got the bread.'

'A long one?'

'Maybe that's not the term you use in the British courts, Miles, but a million dollars is a million dollars by any name you like to use.'

'How do you come to be so well informed?' Brian asked.

'There are certain circles which I frequent,' Ulysses replied suavely, 'where such matters are discussed and I must tell you that your predicament is common knowledge in some of the sleaziest bars in the Bronx and Brooklyn. In Manhattan, your exploits are followed with the keenest interest from the Battery to Harlem.'

'Are you behind this scam?' Lucinda breathed venomously.

'My, aren't you suspicious!' Ulysses laughed. 'No, can't you understand that in this little affray, we are on the same side? Your brainless poop of a father has been taken by one of the most accomplished and unscrupulous con men in the game. I admire the way that you have tried to build up a commercial sex business to get you out of the grasp of old Herbie Weissbein.'

'Our man is called Hiram T. Watergate,' protested Gerald.

'Herbie Weissbein, Hiram Watergate, Horace T. Washington and a dozen others – different names, same guy.'

'And what do you want from us in return for your help? The island of Xanthos and its heather?'

Ulysses shook his head. 'I want nothing from you. Dealing with Herbie will give me great pleasure. You see, quite a long time ago, I had some business with him – I won't bore you with the details which I am sure you would consider sordid. Anyway, we were partners and Herbie-Hiram double-crossed me. Getting even with him has been one of my ambitions for years and because of your present difficulties, I have a scheme, ready made. Take it from me, this guy is a professional and without me, you stand no chance at all against him. Didn't someone once talk about using devils to cast out other devils? Well, regard me as your own family demon. Of course, when we have dealt with your problem, if you care to give me some of that heather juice for which I would find a ready use, as a token of your gratitude, I would not be so bad mannered as to refuse. But that's entirely up to you. What I really want is to settle my score with horrible Herbie.'

'And do you know this Contessa who is in with him?'

'Contessa!' Ulysses chuckled. 'The Countess of Jersey City. Sure, I know that broad, and I know exactly how to use her. So, what about it? I am a pretty accomplished con man myself. Are you ready to do things my way?'

He gave them the confident smile of the only water seller in the Sahara Desert.

Miles shrugged his shoulders. 'I don't see that we have much choice,' he said with a glance at the others who glumly nodded their agreement. 'What do you propose?'

'That's my boy!' smiled his uncle. 'What we need is an expedition against Herbie in his base – a sort of strike force in stealth. I want Lucinda and Brian to come with me to New York. And bring a good supply of that heather liquor with you. Miles and Sarah can stay here and keep your sex fun-fair going as a diversion. Also, try to stop that sucker of a Viscount from making any other smart deals.'

'That's fine with me,' said Lucinda. 'When do we start?'

'Just as soon as you have got packed and have that passion juice ready. We have a hell of a lot to do and not much time.'

'So, let's get moving,' Brian urged.

Ulysses Blake, the black sheep of the family, was back home in the fold.

PART III

'Naked she lay; clasped in my longing arms,
I filled with love, and she all over charms;
Both equally inspired with eager fire,
Melting through kindness, flaming in desire.
With arms, legs, lips close clinging to embrace,
She clips me to her breast, and sucks me to her face
Her nimble tongue, Love's lesser lightning played
Within my mouth, and to my thoughts conveyed
Swift orders that I should prepare to throw
The all-dissolving thunderbolt below.'

(The Imperfect Enjoyment)
JOHN WILMOT, EARL OF ROCHESTER

CHAPTER 8

There are quite a number of dignified residences in Westchester County which provide a welcome relief from the noise polluted hysteria of New York City. One such building, an old fashioned, sprawling mansion, housed the Deare Center. It stood at the end of a short driveway, among a cluster of rather untidy rhododendron bushes. A sharp eyed observer one misty morning might have caught a glimpse of a sprightly gentleman in a tweed suit and wearing a cloth cap, crouching in one of the bushes, gazing intently at the Deare Center through a pair of binoculars. Ulysses Blake had set out to reconnoitre the enemy position before launching his attack.

There is not a lot that can be discovered about a refuge for the mentally distraught from the vantage point of a rhododendron bush, apart from possible places for a break-in, but Ulysses had insisted that casing the joint was a necessary opening gambit. However, he was aware of this limitation and had planned a penetration in depth. Even the most short sighted observer would have noticed Brian, more formally dressed and carrying a brief-case, striding along the drive and ringing the bell at the front door.

Ulysses' plan had been for Brian to get into the clinic and gather as much information as possible about the layout and the inmates. To that end, he had assumed the role of a salesman, seeking to interest the administration of the Deare Center in a new line of disposable bed-sheets for which he had assembled a collection of brochures.

Ulysses' reconnaissance failed to achieve its objective. A young girl had answered the door and was on the point of ushering Brian into the Center when a well-built but flashily dressed blonde appeared at the doorway on her way out. As Brian had never seen her before, he was not able to recognize the notoricus Contessa de Scarpio, but Ulysses, peering through his glasses, had no difficulty in identifying Semiramide.

'What does this bum want?' she demanded of the maid.

'I have a very useful article to show whoever it is who is responsible for ordering your supplies and equipment here,' Brian informed her with a winning smile. He patted his brief-case encouragingly. 'It's a disposable bed-sheet for the incontinent,' he added, in a confidential tone.

'Beat it,' Semiramide ordered. 'Our patients are not incontinent, whatever that may mean.'

'They don't have to wet the bed,' Brian pleaded. 'Quite ordinary people can use the sheets. You just throw them away when you have finished sleeping or whatever else you might do in the bed.'

If Brian hoped that this afterthought might convince Semiramide, he was doomed to disappointment. At that moment, they were joined by Hiram T. Watergate himself, also on his way out of the clinic. When Brian's mission was explained to him, Hiram was even more emphatic than his colleague in inviting Brian to leave.

'On your way,' Hiram dismissed Brian and turned to Semiramide. 'Listen,' he told her, 'I guess I won't be able to make our date tonight. I have a dinner with old Mrs Beckmesser. With a little tact and persuasion, she might become one of our patrons and, is that dame loaded!'

'Gee, that's a shame,' Semiramide complained. 'I particularly wanted to go to The Black Cockatoo tonight. You know they have that black jazz pianist, Paul Lincoln. He's terrific.'

'Well, why don't you go anyway?' Hiram replied. 'Then, if I get through with Frau Beckmesser early, I can come and join you.'

'I guess I'll do that,' Semiramide said.

'Christ, are you still here!' Hiram shouted at Brian, who had loitered in order to overhear this conversation. 'I thought I told you to get your ass moving.'

Brian gulped. 'I just wanted to tell you that we have a special line in paper towels since you weren't that struck by the sheets –'

'If you are not out of here by the time I have counted to one,' Hiram interrupted, 'I'll have the cops on you.'

'O.K.' Brian shrugged his shoulders and turned away. 'You don't know what a bargain you are missing,' he called as he retreated.

Lucinda was waiting in the midtown Manhattan hotel which the trio had adopted as their headquarters. Brian got back there and helped himself to a drink, as he settled down to wait for Ulysses. Lucinda's uncle had shrunk back into the bushes as Brian walked back up the drive and he remained under cover until Hiram and Semiramide had left and were well on their way. Then, he too, made his way back to the hotel and the consolation of a stiff Bourbon.

'So, how did you make out?' Lucinda asked.

'I can't pretend that the expedition was a great success,' Ulysses confessed. 'Apart from finding out the colour of the wallpaper when the door was opened to young Brian, I didn't glean much information on Fort Deare. Just as Brian ought to have infiltrated and started to do his stuff,

Hiram and Semiramide appeared and turned him out. We really are no further forward. We must try to find out what their routine is – what they do and where they go. I have an idea, but it means getting Semiramide on her own.'

'Well, she'll be on her own tonight,' Brian told him, and he recounted the conversation between Hiram and Semiramide which he had overheard.

'The Black Cockatoo,' mused Ulysses. 'Maybe this will turn out to be our lucky day after all.'

The Black Cockatoo was the 'in place' for jazz devotees in Greenwich Village. It was a friendly bar, decorated with an array of stuffed parrots of every colour except black. There was a crowd around the counter, drinking beers or soft drinks and not all the smoke which hung heavy in the air came from tobacco. Brian and Lucinda had got there early and found a table in a corner where they devoured the statutory hamburger, lingered over a lager and awaited the arrival of Semiramide. Music blared from a tape player behind the bar but shortly before half past ten it was abruptly switched off and a tall, muscular, black man with tight curly hair and a strangely diffident air, took his place at the piano. At almost the same moment, Brian caught sight of Semiramide as she pushed her way through the throng at the bar.

'That's her,' he told Lucinda. 'I'll call Ulysses.'

Taking care to keep well away from his quarry just in case she recognized him, Brian slipped out, found a phone and summoned Ulysses, who was waiting in the hotel.

By the time he got back to the table, Paul Lincoln had started to play. He had a style that was all his own, a strange mixture of old fashioned New Orleans, raucous honky-tonk and something of the finger fleet arabesques of an Oscar Peterson. Lucinda was listening, spellbound and when Brian went to speak to her, she silenced him until the music stopped.

'Isn't he terrific?' she enthused.

'Pretty good,' Brian answered airily. 'But you should be keeping your eye on Semiramide not ogling some hunk of ebony who hits the ivories.'

'I can see her. She hasn't moved,' Lucinda told him crossly. 'Now, shut up, he's going to start playing again.'

Paul Lincoln caressed a sad blues out of the keys. The crowded bar grew quiet as the magic of his music got through and Lucinda was so absorbed that she never noticed the entry of Ulysses and only realized that he had arrived when she saw him, sitting at the table with Semiramide.

Semiramide also had been concentrating on the music and was taken by surprise when she found, sitting beside her, a figure from the better forgotten past.

'Why aren't you hiding under some stone, a long way from here?' she snarled.

Ulysses favoured her with a benevolent smile. 'Glad to hear that you have kept your old, sweet nature, Frankie, darling. Or should I call you Semiramide?'

'Drop dead, creep!'

'Anything to oblige, but there are a few things I need to do first.' Ulysses gave her arm an affectionate pat. 'As a matter of fact,' he continued, 'I have been looking for you. I have a little proposition to put to you.'

'Who are you kidding?' Semiramide bristled.

'I am serious. I have a beautiful set-up: it's a steal – and a lot of money simply waiting for a couple like you and me to take it. That's the point, Frankie, to lift this deal, I need a woman, but she has to be really good. Now, I remember how you and Herbie took me a long time ago. As far as I am concerned that's all over: I've made enough since then not to bear a grudge. But, you were great, the best – and that's what I need.'

'I'm busy.'

'Too busy to take a couple of hundred thousand dollars for a few days' work?'

'How much?'

'You heard, honey. And you will still be able to cash in on whatever Herbie is prepared to slip you for his little caper.'

Sincerity shone from Ulysses' bright blue eyes. Semiramide regarded him with a renewed interest. She was torn between suspicion and avarice: as was usually the case, avarice won.

'Is this on the level?' she demanded.

'You have my word.' Ulysses put on his grave expression, looking like some mediaeval pope, granting absolution to a repentant sinner. 'Why else would I have scoured this wretched city to find you?'

'So, what's the big deal?'

'I can't discuss it here. Can we go back to your place?'

'I came here to hear the music.'

'Two hundred thousand dollars,' Ulysses reminded her.

'Let's go.' Semiramide was on her feet and, grabbing her coat, led the way out of The Black Cockatoo.

Ulysses followed her without a glance at Lucinda and Brian but, behind his back he gave them a thumbs-up.

'Well, that seems O.K.' Brian said with a grim smile. 'Shall we go?'

'I want to stay and hear this guy play some more,' Lucinda replied.

'I'd like to go and get something decent to eat,' Brian grumbled. 'Those hamburgers are lethal.'

'You go off, then, and have a meal. I'll see you back at the hotel.'

'I don't like leaving you here alone.'

'Don't be ridiculous.' Lucinda was annoyed. 'What sort of a woman do you think I am? I can look after myself without a male minder. Off you go and fill your rumbling belly.'

Brian looked at her dubiously, but got up and walked slowly to the exit. When he had passed through the door, Lucinda left her table and found a seat beside the piano. The young pianist glanced up and gave her a friendly smile as she sat down.

Meanwhile Ulysses and Semiramide had taken a cab and were heading towards her apartment near the park.

'So, what's this big deal?' she demanded.

'Wait until we get to your place,' Ulysses told her. 'Then, I won't describe it, I'll actually give you a demonstration.'

This did not satisfy Semiramide and Ulysses steadfastly refused to discuss the matter for the rest of the ride.

At last, they arrived. No sooner were they through the front door than Semiramide, thoroughly bad tempered by now, renewed her attack.

'O.K., smart ass! We're here, so give!'

'Nice little place you have.' Ulysses smiled approvingly, as he looked around him. 'Furnished in your characteristically impeccable bad taste, but the view is terrific.'

The apartment was on the twenty-fifth floor and far below them, Manhattan twinkled and glowed in a shrouded silence. Semiramide furiously strode across the room, pressed a button and electrically operated curtains glided across the window, shutting out the romantic vision.

'Let's get down to business, you bum!' invited the lady.

With a sigh, Ulysses turned away from the vanished prospect and took his place on a pink, plastic, near-genuine, Regency sofa. He took in the decor with a shudder.

'What's the hurry? We have the whole night before us. Now, go and fix us a couple of drinks and then come and sit here beside me. You will be truly amazed at what I have in store for you.'

'Business first, drinks later,' snapped Semiramide.

'No drinkee, no talkee,' answered Ulysses complacently and he folded his arms and waited.

'Holy shit!' exclaimed his gracious hostess, but she went to a concealed bar and produced a couple of bottles and glasses.

'You have the choice,' she informed him, 'Scotch and Coke or Coke and Scotch.'

'Just pour us a little Coke. I have something in my hip flask which you ought to try.'

'I'm not thirsty.'

'Taste it anyway: I'd like to know what you think of it. It's a local liqueur which I picked up on my travels and I assure you that it really packs a punch. So, let's drink to our partnership. May it prosper and make us obscenely rich!'

The last appeal got through to Semiramide who, having dispensed the Coke, took the glass into which Ulysses had poured a finger of a liquid from the flask which he had taken from his pocket. Ulysses eyed the big, blowzy blonde with distaste and then, with an air of resignation which would have done credit to one of the early martyrs, added a shot of the liquid to his own drink.

'Happy days,' Semiramide wished him, as she gulped down her drink.

'Tormented nights, more likely,' muttered her guest, sipping his potion apprehensively.

'So, now, let's get down to your proposition,' Semiramide persisted.

'What do you think of the drink?' asked Ulysses, desperately playing for time for the heather juice to work.

'Quit fooling! If you have something to offer, get it off your chest, brother. Otherwise – out!' And she jerked her thumb expressively towards the door.

'The reason I asked you what you thought of the booze,' Ulysses informed her mildly, 'is because that is the proposition.'

'What are you talking about?'

'The answer to all our problems was the stuff I poured into your glass.'

Semiramide gazed at him in bewilderment which turned to horror. 'Have you poisoned me?'

'Don't be silly. You saw I drank some of the hooch as well and I would hardly have gone to all this trouble to set up a suicide pact with you. Tell me, don't you feel something?'

'What sort of something?'

'Wait a moment. You'll know when it arrives.'

'Say, Ulysses Blake, if this is some sort of joke, I'll . . .'

Semiramide never indicated exactly what horrible vengeance she proposed to wreak on her nonchalant bootlegger. She stopped in the middle of her threat and regarded Ulysses, open mouthed. A new gleam came into her eyes and she uttered a loud gasp.

'Shall we head towards your bedroom?' Ulysses suggested. He had purposely taken only a fraction of the dose which he administered to Semiramide but he felt the unmistakable pangs of lust.

When he had walked out of The Black Cockatoo, Brian had also complained of pangs, but his were of hunger. However, as he paced the sidewalk, debating whether to indulge himself in Italian pasta or a huge American T-bone steak, he found that his appetite was diminishing.

He had been piqued by the way Lucinda had apparently preferred the company of an unknown pianist in a dingy bar to his own. It was a blow to his pride but worse, Brian realized with a shock that he was suffering from that most insidious of all maladies, jealousy. And all over nothing, he told himself. Lucinda had not even exchanged one word with the fellow. But, somehow, he was not convinced and, after a half hearted attempt at a meal, he walked back, in a miserable frame of mind, to the hotel.

Actually, his doubts had some justification. Back in The Black Cockatoo, Paul Lincoln had noticed the pretty chick who had taken her place near the piano and he definitely approved. She seemed to have a style which you didn't find among the denizens of The Black Cockatoo or the other Village hang-outs. He finished the blues with a dreamy, unresolved chord and turned towards her with a smile.

'Did you like that?' he asked.

'It was great,' Lucinda answered. 'You really are good: do you play here every night?'

'Just two or three times a week. I am studying music and I need the money for my tuition fees.'

Several other people came over to talk to Paul and Lucinda got up to make room for them.

Paul turned to her and said, 'Don't go away. I have to do another three or four numbers and then I'll be through for the evening. We could grab a bite to eat and talk a little – that is, if you would like to?'

'I'd like it very much,' answered Lucinda and she settled down to wait for her new friend.

At about the same time, Ulysses was fully occupied with his old enemy, for that was how he classed Semiramide ever since their previous encounter. But his plan for dealing with Hiram hinged on turning her against Hiram, with the aid of the heather aphrodisiac and splitting up their alliance. She was certainly proving responsive to treatment.

'Fuck me,' she ordered, as she dragged him into her bedroom.

'I thought you wanted to discuss business,' Ulysses reminded her.

'Fuck business: fuck me,' she screamed.

'Now, let's get this absolutely straight,' Ulysses spoke in the measured tones of a slow-witted lawyer from Hicksville, 'the little matter of two hundred thousand dollars is no longer of interest to you?'

Semiramide was foaming with impatience and was ripping off her clothes.

'Quit stalling and give it to me!' she panted.

Ulysses shook his head sadly, but he started to remove his trousers.

'You never were much good at foreplay,' he commented drily.

Semiramide could not wait for him to finish his leisurely disrobing. Already naked herself, she threw him onto the bed and tugged at his remaining garments.

'Steady,' he cautioned. 'That shirt came from Brookes Brothers.'

Ulysses was sporting a healthy erection and Semiramide went to seize his penis and insert it in her aching vagina but he squirmed out of her grasp.

'You know you gave me a hard time just now. Not at all what I would call a friendly reception.'

'I'm sorry,' she said hastily, making another grab which Ulysses evaded.

'Saying sorry isn't good enough,' he admonished. 'You will have to be very nice to me before I forgive you.'

'What do you want?' Her voice was hoarse.

'Well, for a start, you can treat my vital organs with the sort of respect they merit.'

To emphasize the point, Ulysses gave his cock a gentle pat, pointed it at her and commanded her brusquely,

'Kiss it!'

Obediently, Semiramide sank to her knees and took the full length of his member into her mouth. She kissed it, she sucked it, she slid her tongue all over it and gently played with the throbbing blue vein. At length, she looked up at Ulysses hopefully, but he shook his head.

'More!' he ordered.

Semiramide clasped his buttocks and gratefully licked his balls while Ulysses leaned back on the bed. Despite his apparent detachment, he was also feeling the effect of the heather nectar which he had drunk and he knew that he could not hold out much longer. But, first of all he had to attend to a little business and he summoned all his will power.

'Frankie,' he said quietly but firmly, 'I am not at all pleased with the way you are behaving.'

'Aren't I giving you a swell blow job?' she pleaded.

Ulysses shook his head. 'I am referring to your association with that piece of excrement in human shape, Herbie.'

'Can't we forget Herbie and get a bit of action here?' she entreated, pointing between her legs.

'If you want more of that juice when the effect of the drop you took has worn off, you will have to play along with me – and I am out to get Herbie just where I want him. So, are you going to co-operate?'

'Anything you say,' Semiramide replied meekly. 'I tell you, Ulysses, Herbie is nothing to me. Our relationship was purely commercial. But you've got to give it to me now, Ulysses. Please, please,' her voice rose in a pitiful crescendo, 'I'll do whatever you want – I promise, but fuck me, now, now, now!'

'Don't you forget it,' Ulysses told her, as he moved over and made room for her on the bed.

In an instant, Semiramide had clambered onto the bed and straddled Ulysses who was on his back and who had no chance to react. With a scream of relief and wild pleasure, she forced herself down and plunged his shaft, hard as granite, strong as steel and as hot as her own fevered blood, deep, deep into her. She rode him savagely, her pussy swallowing his fine, firm cock as avidly as, a few minutes earlier, her mouth had done. But, so great was her agitation that she succumbed to a quaking orgasm after only about a dozen strokes and she fell, exhausted, sobbing on Ulysses' prone body.

Yet this fulfilment brought no respite to the racing of her blood and the unquenchable thirst which seemed to torment the very centre of her being. Ulysses himself was now thoroughly aroused and he kissed her passionately while she lay, inert and panting. Then, laying her on her back, he penetrated her easily and swiftly, for she was drenched. As he thrust his penis into her yielding warmth, he could still feel the final tremors of her vagina.

But Semiramide had great powers of recuperation. As Ulysses moved up and down, he felt her beginning to respond and to move to his rhythm. Her smell was strong and raunchy, but he drank it in as if it were the perfume of a goddess. His hands were kneading her lavishly generous breasts and he joined his mouth to hers in a frantic, sensual embrace.

As he felt his own climax approaching, Ulysses, the sensuous artist, wanted to hold back and prolong that marvellous moment but there was no restraining the frenzy of Semiramide.

'Don't stop,' she cried. 'Give me everything you have, baby! Now, now, every drop!'

All her muscles tightened and she held him to her, a prisoner within the lush depths of her body. At the moment of his ejaculation, she came again herself with the same wild throbbing which engulfed all her senses.

They both lay, shattered and spent, fighting for breath, still folded in each other's arms. Then, once more, they began to make love but, at least to start with, in a more placid and controlled manner. A sense of wonder and refinement came into their caresses and they performed a fantastic ballet of desire and enjoyment. Over and over again, they explored each other's bodies, stroking and kissing every sweet swelling or lovely hollow. Ulysses had never loved this woman, but he was able to savour with an intensity he had never before imagined, the glorious, full roundness of her ass, the delicate tracery of the veins in her great breasts and the feline grace of her limbs. For her part, Semiramide's passion was more concentrated and less subtle. She simply needed his cock inside her – in her cunt, in her mouth, in her ass, anywhere and everywhere.

Several times they paused to take a drink and come up for air but after a few minutes' rest, they would start again with renewed vigour. Ulysses did not need to remind Semiramide of her promise: she was completely under his control, doting on him, virtually enslaved.

Eventually, they were overcome by sheer fatigue and fell into a deep but fitful sleep. Ulysses was the first to recover and, in the morning he made himself a coffee, left the apartment and made his way back to the hotel, leaving Semiramide fast asleep, snoring contentedly and oblivious to the world.

Brian's evening was a much tamer affair than that of Ulysses. Back in the hotel, he waited for the return of

Lucinda. He watched some TV but soon got bored and he found no consolation in either reading or listening to the radio. Time passed, but there was no sign of Lucinda. Brian realized bitterly that Paul Lincoln must have stopped playing the piano at The Black Cockatoo long ago. He was too miserable to go to bed but he took a couple of drinks and fell asleep in the small hours, huddled up on a sofa, a book on his lap, the table lamp still burning.

As for Lucinda, it was quite late before Paul was finally able to make his escape from The Black Cockatoo.

'I'm sorry that you had to wait so long,' he said as they came out onto the street.

'That's all right. I didn't have anything special to do tonight.'

'I thought that you were with some guy when you first came into the bar?'

'Just a friend,' Lucinda smiled. 'Where are we going?'

'There's a place I know that's open almost all night. It's nothing elaborate but if you don't mind settling for a steak and a salad?'

'That's fine with me.'

The restaurant turned out to be only a few blocks away from The Black Cockatoo. There were some other late customers, a couple of taxi drivers and three or four students who, like Paul, worked at nights.

'So, do you always pick up foreign girls who listen to your playing?' asked Lucinda.

'Only if they are beautiful. And that happens all too rarely. And do you go out with any struggling student who invites you?'

'Only if they are handsome,' laughed Lucinda. 'And that does not come about very often also.'

'Well, now we understand each other, tell me about yourself. What are you doing in New York anyway?'

Lucinda felt attracted to the young, black pianist. She had a strong hunch that he was somebody who could be trusted, but she resisted the temptation to explain her mission and the crusade against Hiram T. Watergate.

'I am staying with my uncle who has some business to deal with in New York,' she answered semi-truthfully.

They chatted easily and when it was time to leave, Paul took Lucinda's hand and said to her:

'You know, I get the feeling that you have some serious problem which you haven't told me. I can't explain it, but I am sensitive to the way some people with whom I am in sympathy behave. You have a sort of tension beneath the surface. I can't put it any clearer than that. I've taken a liking to you, Lucinda, and I tell you most sincerely, if there is any way I can be of help to you, just call on me.'

Lucinda was taken by surprise. Paul was gazing at her intently and with a serious expression on his face. The conviction that she had found an ally on whom she could depend was overwhelming.

'You certainly are a perceptive young man,' she said with a smile. 'Maybe I shall let you into my dark secret some day and take up your offer.'

'I'll give you a number where you can always contact me.' Paul wrote on a scrap of paper which he handed to Lucinda. 'In any case, I hope we can see each other again.'

'You can depend on it,' Lucinda told him.

He had escorted her back to the hotel but she knew intuitively that he did not expect her to ask him in. She kissed him lightly and hurried into the lobby. Paul watched her vanish inside the impersonal vastness of the hotel and then he slowly walked away. There was something about that girl which had got through to him, some sort of harmony between them which had prompted him to speak as he had done. He was sure that she would call him, not out of any sense of conceit, but from a deep understanding of the kind of person that he knew Lucinda to be.

Up in their suite, Lucinda saw Brian stretched out on the sofa, sound asleep. She decided against waking him. For some reason, after her evening with Paul, she felt the need to be alone, so she tiptoed into the bedroom, undressed in the dark and climbed into bed.

She was awakened next morning by the sound of voices. Slipping on a robe, she went into the salon and witnessed Brian, stiff from his cramped sleep, greeting the wreck of what had once been her Uncle Ulysses.

'I have sacrificed my manhood for the cause,' croaked Ulysses, as he tottered into a chair. 'Don't stare at me as if I were already a ghost: just bring me a cup of hot, black coffee and administer the last rites.'

Brian turned his gaze to Lucinda. His eyes were cold and there was bitterness in his voice.

'I presume that you have enjoyed your night on the town. It was nice of you to get back for breakfast.'

'Don't be ridiculous: I've been in for hours. Do you think that I was parading through the streets of New York in my nightdress?'

'I never heard you come in,' Brian argued.

'Of course not. You had passed out on the sofa with an empty glass and a bottle of Scotch beside you. If you had not been in such a hurry to get away to fill your stomach, you could have spent the rest of the evening with us and had a good time.'

'Us? Does that mean that you went home with that Greenwich Village gigolo?'

'As a matter of fact, I did not but maybe next time I'll do just that. You don't own me, you know, Brian.'

He snorted in barely suppressed rage. Lucinda herself was trembling with anger.

'I suppose the next thing will be that you will be hopping into bed with the guy,' hissed Brian.

'Why not? He's probably a damned sight better fuck than you are,' she retorted.

'Please, don't use that word in my presence,' moaned Ulysses. 'I never want to hear, see, smell or feel a fuck again for the rest of what is left of my sadly shortened life.'

The other two seemed to resent having their quarrel interrupted and regarded him as if he were some loathsome reptile which had crept into their lives.

'Goddammit!' Ulysses exploded. 'All I ask for is a black coffee. And will you please stop bickering like a couple of stupid kids. I am the guy who has been working his ass off. And, let me tell you, I am the guy who has got results. You are supposed to be helping me fix Herbie-Hiram, not getting all het up over some part-time piano player.'

Lucinda went to a phone and ordered from room service some breakfast for herself and the life restoring fluid for Ulysses.

'You can order what you like,' she informed Brian. Then, turning to Ulysses, she asked,

'Are we to take it from your condition that you and the fake Contessa have had a ball?'

'Don't talk about balls either,' complained Ulysses. 'I think that I shall donate mine to some Museum of Medical Marvels as the most overworked organs in the annals of the human race. They ache,' he added and looked around him for sympathy.

'You'll probably find that you are in competition with this Paul Lincoln character,' sneered Brian.

Lucinda ignored the innuendo and waited for Ulysses to recount his heroic saga.

His blow by blow (and suck by suck) account was interrupted by the arrival of breakfast. Refreshed, he began to show symptoms of survival.

'Believe me,' he boasted, 'I have got this thing sewn up. Frankie, or Semiramide as you insist on calling her, has been conquered and from now on, she will work with us against Herbie. With a traitor in his camp, we've got him cold.'

'How can you be so sure?' asked Brian.

'Brother, you should have seen that dame when I left her. She is completely besotted with me. I tell you, I gave her a mammoth sized shot of heather nectar and she is hooked on the stuff.'

He regarded his audience in triumph.

'Now, if you two will stop your petty vendetta,' he told them, 'we can get down to planning our campaign. All right?'

'You are quite right,' Lucinda said. 'You have done splendidly: we ought to be grateful.' And she kissed him on the cheek.

Ulysses was sufficiently recovered that he took the embrace without wincing.

'I'm sorry I blew my top,' Brian apologized shamefacedly. 'I guess that there's no reason for me to get that jealous about a fellow we might never see again.'

'You're forgiven,' replied Lucinda.

But she was pretty sure that she, at any rate, would be seeing more of Paul Lincoln before too long.

CHAPTER 9

Readers of the chronicle of Lucinda's exploits on the island of Xanthos will recall that a stiff dose of nectar, unless diluted by fruit juices is marked by a most unfortunate after-effect, namely a hangover of such intensity that it could fell any ox which was so misguided as to imbibe the brew.*

Somewhere around midday, Semiramide was making the unhappy discovery that every night before is succeeded by the morning after. She had the impression that her head had been detached from its moorings and used throughout the previous night as a football. Some well-wisher appeared to have lined her throat with fluffy blotting paper and her eyes felt as if they were rotating independently of each other. The sun was shining but it brought no joy into her life: rather, she was chagrined to observe that the human species had survived the night. She lurched to her feet and waited for the room to stop its giddy motion. Hazy recollections of the previous evening began to seep through the creaking and thumping machine which she housed in her skull and served her as a brain. She commenced to curse the name of Ulysses Blake with a fluency which would have made her the envy of the most foul-mouthed army sergeant and would have brought a blush to the cheeks of Rabelais himself.

---

* Brian, while experimenting with the nectar, had discovered that almost any citrus fruit in the mix totally banished the monstrous hangovers they had experienced in Xanthos.

He appropriately christened his cocktail the 'Power Screwdriver'.

She was interrupted in this activity by the deafening clamour of a tocsin, a clanging of every bell in every steeple in the State. She would never have believed that her telephone could emit such an ear-splitting din.

She grabbed the receiver and greeted the unknown caller with the words,

'Whoever you are, drop dead!'

She was on the point of replacing the offending instrument when she heard the plaintive voice of Hiram, addressing her.

'Holy cow, what's got into you? I was calling to say that I was sorry that I never got away last night in time to see you at The Black Cockatoo. Maybe I was lucky if your evening put you into that sort of temper.'

'I've got a headache,' she mumbled.

'You've got a sore head,' he corrected. 'Call me back when you feel more communicative.'

He hung up and Semiramide looked blankly at the lifeless telephone for a minute before drifting into the kitchen and taking a couple of neat aspirins.

Slowly, her mental functions returned to something approaching normal and with each moment of clearer perception, her hatred of Ulysses grew more venomous. She recalled that he had said something about getting even with Hiram and he was going to use her as an accomplice. In the cold light of day, this did not seem a good idea.

However, she realized that Ulysses had something like dynamite in his hip flask. The more she considered her behaviour, the more she appreciated the potential of that potion. Now, if only she and Hiram could get hold of that stuff, what power would be theirs and what wealth they would be able to command.

She realized that by now, Hiram would be in the Deare Center so she called him there.

'Say, what goes with you?' he demanded testily. 'I thought that you were going to bite my head off.'

'Yeah, I guess I was sort of hasty,' she admitted, 'but I was in a hell of a state. You see, I spent the night with Ulysses Blake.'

'Ulysses? I thought that maybe he had done us a good turn and got himself cremated. And you mean to tell me that you were in the sack with that sucker! That's morbid.'

'I didn't want to, but Ulysses gave me something to drink which made me go crazy. I tell you, man, I couldn't stop fucking.'

Hiram laughed cynically. 'You've never needed an excuse before. So you were horny – what's new in town?'

'I was not horny,' Semiramide declared indignantly. 'At least, not until that louse doped me. Believe me, Hiram, that stuff is sensational. We have to get it away from Ulysses. We can put it to good use.'

'You're out of your mind,' Hiram told her. 'Don't we have enough on our hands with the Center and in a few months, Hamblewood? As long as Ulysses stays out of my way, I'm happy.'

'Well, that's another thing,' Semiramide said slowly. 'It seems that Ulysses has not forgiven you for that trick you pulled on him. He's looking for you.'

'Is that so? I suppose that puts a different complexion on things. O.K., so he has this wonder drug? What do you propose?'

'I thought that if we could get him on his own, you might be able to persuade him to part with the hooch, or whatever it is. Some of the big fellows you have knocking around can be mighty persuasive.'

'I'll arrange a reception committee for Ulysses this afternoon at the Deare Center. I have to be here anyway since I am still working on old Mrs Beckmesser. She's coming over to see the place. Find some reason to bring Ulysses here after she has left.'

Semiramide was considering how to entice Ulysses to the Center when he phoned.

'And how is my sex bomb this morning?' he enquired. 'Are you willing and eager to tackle Herbie, the way we agreed last night?'

'Oh, sure, anything you say,' she assured him.

'So, where is Herbie?'

'Right now, he's out of town.'

'Is that so.'

Ulysses frowned. He had never had a great deal of faith in Semiramide's veracity but the glibness of her lie put him on his guard.

'Any idea when he'll be back?'

'In a few days. Say, Ulysses,' Semiramide was seized by an inspiration. 'Why don't we get together and work out a plan before he gets back to town?'

'Uh huh. Do you have any suggestion?'

'Sure. This afternoon I have to be at a joint called the Deare Center. Why don't you come by, say about five?'

'The Deare Center,' Ulysses mused. 'What sort of a place would that be?'

'It's a clinic.'

'Are you sick?'

'No, Ulysses, nothing like that. I do what you might call a little social work there.'

'I've never thought of you as a social worker, Frankie. That doesn't sound your style.'

'It pays. Don't get any wrong ideas. This is a menagerie of rich dames with open chequebooks.'

'That figures. I wouldn't like to get the impression that my Frankie was being less than frank with me.'

'Gee, Ulysses! How could you suspect anything like that? I mean, after last night.'

Ulysses assiduously took down the address of the Deare Center and directions how to get there. He promised to keep the date: Semiramide swore her undying devotion to him and then hung up.

'That low-down, two faced, lying, double-crossing, two-timing snake in the grass,' commented Ulysses.

'Are we to take it that your adoring slave has raised the flag of revolt?' asked Lucinda gravely.

'It just goes to show that you can never trust a woman,' her uncle confided. 'It was lucky that neither of them spotted me at the Center, yesterday.'

'You are not going to keep that appointment, are you,' said Brian. 'It's obviously a trap.'

'On the contrary, I most certainly am,' Ulysses stated. He was interrupted by the phone.

It was Semiramide. 'I forgot to say, Ulysses, do bring along some more of that marvellous dope, darling. I could do with a bit of a lift.'

'That settles it,' Ulysses told Brian. 'She and Herbie are going to try and snatch the nectar. I'm going to pay my respects to the Deare Center and, while I am inside, you and Lucinda will provide a small diversion among the patients.'

'I have a feeling that this is when we call up reinforcements,' Lucinda said. She took a piece of paper from her bag and called the number which was written on it.

Paul was delighted to hear from Lucinda so soon and hurried over to the hotel to learn what mission the lady had in store for him. Ulysses greeted him with the enthusiasm of a professional conspirator who had found a heaven-sent ally: Brian was rather more surly but he had to admit that they were likely to need all the help that they could muster and Paul looked the type who would prove useful if it came to a show-down. The situation was explained to him and a broad grin spread across his face.

'You want my help? You've got it,' he promised.

So, when shortly before five that afternoon, Ulysses presented himself at the front door of the Deare Center, Lucinda, Brian and Paul were not far away.

Ulysses was shown into a large office. Semiramide was seated in an armchair and she welcomed him with a scowl. Behind a vast desk, smiling sardonically, sat Hiram, a fat cigar between his lips.

'Hi there, Ulysses. It's good to see you again. And you certainly look fit. Let's hope you stay that way.'

'I thought that you were out of town,' said Ulysses in feigned surprise.

'Let's say that I was called back for some unexpected business. Anyway, Westchester County is out of town, isn't it?'

'So, what has sweet, little Frankie been telling you about me?'

Hiram looked at Ulysses appreciatively, rather as a well bred wolf would regard a stray lamb.

'I hear the strangest things,' he replied pensively. 'Like you have some wonder drug that makes women go crazy for you.'

'Come on, Herbie, you know how impressionable Frankie is and I have always possessed great charm. It runs in the family you know.'

Semiramide's patience was exhausted.

'Have you brought that liquor?' she cried.

Ulysses smiled at her smugly but remained silent.

'The lady wants you to hand over this elixir,' Hiram explained. 'She would like me to see how effective it is. Now, I wouldn't want to louse up a friendship as precious as ours by resorting to violence, so I hope that you will part with the stuff, nice and peaceably.'

'And if not, I presume that you will call in a squad of gorillas who are posing as male nurses?'

'Something like that,' replied Hiram affably.

'Don't worry, Herbie,' Ulysses grinned. 'I am only too willing to stage a small scale demonstration of this herbal remedy which has taken Frankie's fancy.'

'Quit stalling, jerk!' ordered the lady. 'Where have you stashed the juice?'

'As I said, I have arranged a demonstration for Herbie's benefit.' Ulysses looked at his watch. 'It should be starting any minute now.'

For a moment, there was silence. Then Hiram made a grimace of resignation.

'You are being very stupid and obstinate,' he chided Ulysses. 'I see that it is necessary to persuade you to do as you are told.'

He pressed a button under his desk. They waited. Nothing happened. With a frown, Hiram pressed the button again, longer and more urgently. Still there was no response to his summons. From outside, however, they heard a confused hubbub. Some men were shouting and there were mingled high pitched screams and giggles. Then there was a crash of some furniture being overturned.

'What the hell is going on?' Hiram howled, jumping to his feet and making for the door.

'Sounds as if the demonstration is going nicely,' Ulysses purred. 'Shall we go and investigate?'

The three of them hurried out of the office.

As soon as Ulysses had been admitted to the Center, Brian and Lucinda went to the front door and rang the bell. The door was opened by the same maid who had been on duty the previous day.

'We're from the World Health Organization,' Brian announced. 'This is a routine inspection.'

The girl looked at him suspiciously.

'Weren't you here yesterday; selling some sort of bed-sheets?' she accused.

'I changed my job,' Brian explained. 'Please show us the rooms which are used as accommodation for your patients.'

'I'm not sure that I ought,' the maid replied nervously. 'You see, the medical staff is off duty and the patients are resting in the Ladies' Lounge and the Gentlemen's Browsery.'

'Browsery?'

'Sure, you know, where they can sit and browse – read books, write letters, pay their accounts at the Center – that sort of thing.'

'Excellent! We can make our inspection without disturbing any doctors or nurses.'

'Are you sure that it will be O.K.? I am not supposed to let in any unauthorized visitors. I could get into trouble.'

'Have you any idea of what sort of trouble you will be in if you refuse admission to representatives of the WHO? We'll have the Center closed.' Lucinda was at her fiercest and most officious.

The unhappy girl submitted before this display of supranational self importance and led them along the corridor.

'The door on the left is the Ladies' Lounge. You will find the gentlemen in the room opposite,' she informed them.

'Thank you. We have no further need of you. You may get on with your work.' Lucinda dismissed her with the curtness of a powerful bureaucrat dealing with some minor problem like bubonic plague or the outbreak of world war.

They had already decided that Lucinda should deal with the men and Brian the women and the unexpected segregation of the lounges made their task easier.

Brian's clientele was the more numerous. He guessed that there were more husbands ready and willing to pay the exorbitant fees of an establishment such as the Deare Center to be rid of the presence of their wives than women who disposed of their mates in the same extravagant fashion. Entering the Ladies' Lounge, he found himself in the midst of a fearsome sample of American matronhood. It took all his resolve not to turn and flee. He produced from his brief-case a large medicine bottle and several plastic cups.

'Ladies,' he announced, 'I have been requested to dispense to you a completely new preparation which has been produced by the most brilliant research chemist of our time specifically for your conditions.'

The assembled women regarded him with interest. Nobody had sold them a patent remedy for hours and they were beginning to feel neglected. Brian began to measure out doses of a colourless liquid into the cups and hand them round.

'Not so fast,' objected a tall woman in her fifties. She had a sharp beak of a nose and the flashing eye of one who is accustomed to command and to be obeyed. 'Are you sure that Dr Holzhammer would approve of my taking this? He is very particular about my treatment.'

'Dr Holzhammer asked me to be certain that you took it,' Brian answered smoothly.

'How do you know?' demanded the gaunt woman sternly. 'Why, you don't even know my name.'

'Dr Holzhammer described you to me. He said the very dignified, good looking lady.'

'In that case, there can't be any doubt,' said the

mollified matriarch and she swallowed the draught in one gulp.

With this break-through, the other patients followed their natural leader without making any difficulties.

'I do hope that it is not constipating,' confided a worried looking, wan creature. 'You have no idea how I suffer.'

'Good Lord, no! It acts as a laxative.'

'Did I hear you say that it is a laxative?' asked a fussy seventy-year-old peroxide blonde. 'I had better not have any. The slightest thing gives me the runs,' she informed Brian with pride.

'It's not that sort of laxative,' he improvised. 'It only has that effect on the constipated. With other people, it works the opposite way. Why, it has even been used as a cure for dysentery.'

While Brian was distributing this panacea to the female population of the Deare Center, Lucinda was performing a similar act of largesse among the males. The first beneficiaries were a couple who were engaged in a game of chess. So intense was their concentration that they swallowed their tonics without even looking up from the board, totally oblivious to her presence. She had more difficulty with a moody customer who was reading a book and didn't want to be disturbed.

'Do take it like a good boy,' Lucinda pleaded. 'Just to please me,'

She adopted her most winning smile and fluttered her eyelashes in mute supplication. Her victim melted. She managed to distribute cups of nectar to another half a dozen more or less able bodied, relaxing men before the noise of a disturbance outside gave warning that in the female quarters, the rutting season had commenced. She dashed into the corridor where she ran into Brian.

'How many have you nobbled?' she called.

'I got to the twelfth when the first of them threw her head back and charged.'

'We should have enough for an eventful afternoon's diversion.'

'Let's hope that your precious pal, Paul, comes up to scratch.'

When Brian had judged that the time had come to make his escape, Dr Holzhammer's prize patient had turned to her chronically constipated companion with an air of amazement.

'Do you know, Abigail,' she exulted, 'I am beginning to feel something I haven't felt for years.'

'It's something I've never experienced before,' her friend confided. 'Shall we join the gentlemen, Hermione?'

'Sure. Unless we can find some glorious hunks of male nurses first.'

This was the signal for a general gallop for the door and Brian and Lucinda skipped aside to avoid being trampled in the stampede or suffering a worse fate.

With a howl of triumph, Hermione swept aside the chess-board and swooped on the man who had been playing White.

'Come on, Basil,' she screamed, 'let's do it!'

Before her startled adversary could react, Abigail had pounced on Black.

'Take me, a demure, young virgin,' she crooned. 'I have been keeping my cherry just for you – or somebody like you.'

Fortunately, the men were also starting to feel the effects of the nectar and they responded positively to the unexpected entreaties of the nymphs. However, as Brian had administered more doses to the women than Lucinda had to the men, in a number of instances, seduction gave way to rape. Pandemonium broke out and the nursing staff who were enjoying their rest hour, hurried to investigate. Outside the Gentlemen's Browsery, they encountered Brian and Lucinda who had been detailed by Ulysses to delay for as long as possible the intervention by the tough bar-bouncers who masqueraded during the days as skilled nurses.

'Don't go in there,' Brian ordered. 'There's nothing to worry about. It's a new form of therapy.'

'It sounds more like a riot,' replied a burly medical assistant with a cauliflower ear.

'That's because it is still in the experimental stage,' Brian explained. 'It renders the patients very excitable. It would be dangerous to interfere with them while they are undergoing this treatment.'

'Dangerous for who?' demanded a man-mountain.

Brian and Lucinda managed to keep up their diversion for some time, but the racket inside continued unabated, and the guardians of the Center were uneasy.

'Say, you,' a man resembling a walking tree addressed Brian. 'Who gave orders for this therapy or whatever it is?'

Brian gave the first name that came into his head.

'Dr Holzhammer,' he replied in an authoritative tone of voice.

'Who are you kidding?' challenged the oak tree. 'I am Dr Holzhammer.'

'Of course you are,' Lucinda interposed. 'Don't you remember your own instructions?'

A minor dispute now erupted between the oak tree called Holzhammer and the other members of the forest but, eventually Holzhammer convinced his colleagues that he was not responsible for the extraordinary revolution in medical science which was taking place. He turned to wreak vengeance on Brian and Lucinda, but they had vanished. The posse of nurses rushed into the Gentlemen's Browsery, an action which, a moment later, they regretted bitterly.

A scene of indescribable confusion met their eyes. They were accustomed to regarding their charges as pillars of American society, leaders of the Moral Majority, Virtue Incarnate. What they beheld was an orgy that would have won the approval of the most dissolute of the late Roman emperors. Before they knew what was happening, Hermione called on her cohorts.

'Girls, look! More men! What are we waiting for?'

With a happy war whoop, she led her sisters into action against the staff.

Consequently, when Hiram attempted to summon his minions to deal with Ulysses, they were far too heavily engaged to respond. So Hiram was in a particularly bad temper when he led Semiramide and Ulysses towards the Gentlemen's Browsery outside which they met Brian and Lucinda.

'Who the hell are you?' Hiram snarled.

'They're my guests,' Ulysses reassured his host.

'Aren't you something to do with bedsheets?' Semiramide asked Brian.

'That was yesterday's special offer,' he said apologetically. 'I'm afraid that we've sold out. But come and see what we have in store for you today.'

From inside the Gentlemen's Browsery there emerged a high pitched shriek.

'Mabel Eberstadt, take your sinful hands off that nice Dr Holzhammer. He's mine: I saw him first.'

'Don't be greedy. He's got enough for the two of us.' The speaker was a mellow contralto, presumably Mabel Eberstadt.

With a cry of rage, Hiram tore open the door and strode into the mêlée.

The centre-piece of the tableau was without doubt the virtuoso display being staged by Hermione and the former White chess-player. Nearby, Abigail crouched doggy fashion while Black serviced her from the rear. Dr Holzhammer was fending off three ravenous harpies who were showing undreamed of reserves of strength. The room was littered with discarded corsets, bras, trusses and miscellaneous underwear,

'I don't believe it,' cried the dumbfounded proprietor of the Center.

'They've been given that stuff,' Semiramide complained. 'Jesus, what a waste!'

Mabel Eberstadt spotted the newcomers.

'Come and join us,' she invited.

'I do hope that you find my demonstration convincing,' Ulysses said to Hiram.

'Are you responsible for this outbreak?' Hiram asked Brian.

'We thought that the sedate citizens could benefit from some entertainment combined with vigorous exercise. What better than a live-show?'

'Or a love-show,' amended Lucinda.

Their discussion was cut short by a throaty gurgle of satisfaction from Hermione who rolled off the spreadeagled chess-player.

'Boy, I needed that,' she gloated.

Hiram pulled himself together and turned to Holzhammer and his hard pressed assistants.

'Get these animals back in their cages,' he ordered. 'And clear up this mess.'

'Would anybody like a refill?' Lucinda invited, waving her bottle of nectar at the mob.

There was a rush towards her but Hiram knocked the bottle from her hand and what was left of the liquid spilled onto the carpet.

'What a waste!' Semiramide repeated.

'You'll regret this,' Hiram angrily shouted at Ulysses.

There was no reply. Taking advantage of the general confusion, Ulysses had glimmered away and was nowhere to be seen.

'He sort of left,' explained Holzhammer.

'I can see that, stupid,' Hiram retorted. 'And you had better throw these two out before they do any more damage.' He jerked his thumb expressively at Brian and Lucinda.

'Don't bother. We can see ourselves out,' Brian assured him hastily.

'It will be a pleasure,' growled Holzhammer, flexing his muscles.

A menacing scowl passed across his face and he advanced on the pair who were making for the door. But he was robbed of his prey.

'My hero!' screeched Hermione and with an Olympic standard leap, she threw her arms around Holzhammer's neck. 'You are the man I have been waiting for all my life.'

By the time Holzhammer had freed himself from her passionate embrace, Brian and Lucinda were safely out of the building and sprinting to where they had parked their car.

Less than a minute later, another figure slipped out of the Deare Center. Hiram and Semiramide had been far too preoccupied with the riot to notice the unobtrusive, young black man who had been quietly photographing the high spots of the orgy. He flitted from one group to another, taking care not to draw attention to himself. By the time that the others had made their exit, Paul Lincoln judged that he had enough material in his camera and he sidled to the front door and left behind him the scene of wild disorder.

Lucinda, Brian and Ulysses were waiting for him in the car. He jumped in and they drove off towards the city as the last spasms of the Battle of Deare Center died away before the onslaught of Holzhammer's heavy squad.

CHAPTER 10

'Did you get some good pictures?' Ulysses asked anxiously.

'Plenty,' laughed Paul. 'I don't think that any of our subjects suffered from under-exposure.'

All four of them were in an exuberant mood as they headed back towards New York.

'What about getting them developed?' Brian enquired. 'I don't suppose that you would want to leave the negatives in any old shop.'

'No way! That could lead to all sorts of problems,' Paul replied. 'But I had thought of that. I am living in a students' hostel and there is a guy in the next room who is a photographic freak. He and I are buddies and I know that he will deal with them for me.'

'And you can trust him?' Ulysses wanted to know.

'Absolutely. I'd trust him with anything – money, hot merchandise, even my best girl.'

Brian approved of Paul's words but he was less happy about the way he was smiling at Lucinda. Ulysses, however, was sticking to practical business.

'When do you think that you can have the prints?'

'He'll be at classes most of today. I guess I shall be able to get them to you tomorrow evening, let's say by nine.'

'You won't bring them to us: we'll collect them. Hiram will be hopping mad and he would be able to trace us to the hotel in a matter of hours. So we are going to move out and go to earth. Are you sure that nobody noticed you while you were busy with your camera?'

'I'm certain,' Paul answered. 'If anyone had seen me they would have tried to stop me, wouldn't they?'

'That's right,' Ulysses assented. 'So, as they don't know that you exist, your hostel will be safe. We'll drop you off there now and one of us will come round tomorrow evening for your porno-folio.'

'Say,' Paul protested, 'if you are moving out, how do I get in touch with you?'

'You don't,' Ulysses told him. 'You wait for us to contact you. The fewer people who know our new address, the better, at least for the next few days.'

'Don't you trust me?' asked Paul. He sounded hurt and resentful.

'I don't even trust myself,' Ulysses snapped, 'so why should I give anybody else the benefit of the doubt? Now, tell me where this hostel is.'

Paul directed them to an old brown-stone house which had been renovated and converted into a lodging for students from a number of colleges. It stood in a neglected corner, close to Washington Square in down town Manhattan.

'I'm on the second floor, room six,' he informed them. 'You don't need to ask at the door; just come straight up. Call me when you are on your way: Lucinda has my number.'

They dropped Paul close to the hostel and drove back

to the hotel. As soon as they arrived, Ulysses checked out while the others started their hurried packing.

'Any forwarding address?' asked the receptionist.

'1600 Pennsylvania Avenue, Washington, DC,' was Ulysses' prompt response.

The receptionist looked puzzled.

'I'm sure that I've come across that address before,' he mused. 'Doesn't somebody else live there?'

'It's a big place,' Ulysses reassured him.

The bill paid, they stowed their luggage in the car.

'So we're off to Washington,' said Brian. 'Isn't that a bit remote for dealing with your pals in the Deare Center?'

Ulysses gazed at him scornfully. 'Are you so dumb as to think that I would leave a genuine forwarding address for the benefit of anyone Herbie might send around to check on us?'

'So who is at 1600 Pennsylvania Avenue?'

'The President of the United States. I suppose there is no reason why a limey should know the postal address of the White House. We are heading for a hide-out I have not far from town. A man who has been in the sort of business in which I have been involved has need of secluded residences which are not known to anybody,' Ulysses remarked.

'From the little we know of your past, that sounds an under-statement,' Lucinda commented. 'And you are the only person who knows this cosy home for retired fugitives from justice?'

'There is one other individual who knows of its existence and who will not be there and never goes there. Now, as the place has been empty for some time, let's stop on the way and get some groceries and a few other home comforts.'

They stocked up at a supermarket, Ulysses ensuring that they would not die of thirst. Then, with him at the wheel, they drove through the apparently interminable residential sprawl of Long Island, an anonymous dot in the stream of traffic. Eventually, the houses began to thin out and patches of green gave to the landscape a slightly more rural character. Nearby, marshes ran down to a sandy sea-shore and a salty tang in the air mingled with the petrol and diesel fumes.

At Sayville, they found themselves in a small town which had grown up at the spot where a ferry linked Long Island with Fire Island, a long, low series of sand dunes on which thousands of holiday homes had been built. Near the ferry terminal, a ramshackle affair of timber, concrete and rusting corrugated iron, there was a huddle of quite opulent bungalows, standing in well kept gardens. Beyond them were a few local stores and a garage cum gas station. Ulysses turned in and crossed the wide expanse of concrete. Hidden behind the garage was a nondescript brick and timber house.

'It's not the White House,' Ulysses nodded at the building, 'but we can stay here undisturbed and nobody is going to vote us out. And we can leave the car at the garage: there are so many parked there every day by commuters, it will never be noticed. The same goes for this part of Sayville in general. Every weekend, there is such an exodus over to Fire Island that a regiment of Chinese infantry could pass through without attracting any attention from the residents.'

They clambered out and unloaded the car. Ulysses opened the front door and they filed inside.

Dusk had already fallen and when Ulysses had switched on the light, they found themselves in a lounge which was simply but comfortably furnished.

'The place could do with a dusting,' Ulysses observed, running his hand over the pine mantelshelf. 'I was here a few weeks ago but before that it stood empty for years. It's no palace: there are only a couple of bedrooms but I don't suppose you will object to sharing.'

'How long have you had the house then?' Lucinda asked.

'It's been in the family since the days when your grandfather was struggling to make his first million. In those days, Sayville was a quiet country village; all the shanties have grown up much more recently and the place has gone downhill. But we never sold the house, even when the family had gone up in the world and we have always thought of it as some sort of refuge, a retreat where nobody would barge in if we needed time to think or we were in any trouble.'

'We?' queried Lucinda.

'Well,' her uncle laughed, 'although the house belongs to the family, I reckon that I have the monopoly of that sort of trouble. Everybody is respectable except rascally, old Ulysses, so I am the only one to use it.'

It was a fine, warm evening and when they had put their things in their rooms and washed and changed, Lucinda suggested that they take a walk.

'You go with Brian,' Ulysses said. 'I feel like taking it easy. Why don't you go over to the island? There are still ferries running and you can walk for miles along the beach.'

One of the heavy, ungainly craft was on the point of leaving and Lucinda and Brian scuttled up the gangplank seconds before it cast off. The crossing barely lasted for ten minutes: the long, low outline of Fire Island was clearly visible as they pulled away from the Sayville landing stage. The skyline was dominated by dense woods which added a touch of mystery to the otherwise banal landscape. The ferry rounded a protruding spit of land and they were suddenly entering a bay, lined with chalets, boat-houses and a sprinkling of small stores. This was The Pines, the best known and the most fashionable of the resorts which were strung out along Fire Island like beads on a string. Among the trees, there stood solid, well built timber beach houses, connected by a board walk which was laid over the fine sand.

Once ashore, they walked away from the diminutive landing stage along a path which passed between some of the houses. The island was only a few hundred yards wide and in minutes, they had breasted the gentle slope and descended to where the trees gave way to the dunes. Sparse tussocks of grass and weeds waved in the breeze blowing from the expanse of the ocean beyond the broad beach of fine, light sand, glowing a rich gold in the light of the setting sun.

The air smelt good and clean and they walked in silence for a few minutes, relaxing to the hypnotic crashing of the waves breaking on the shore and the hissing of the sand as the water receded. Brian took Lucinda's hand and pulled her close to him.

They did not have the place to themselves. A few of the bolder spirits were retreating from the sea, shivering from their swim. A number of young men and women were enjoying the last of the sun. Most of them were nude, their bodies as brown as gingerbread, and some of them were uninhibitedly making love, stretched on towels or on the warm carpet of dry sand.

They passed a tiny headland. Fewer people were on this more remote beach but a thin wisp of smoke was rising from behind some low dunes where the sand met the advance guard of the intrusive forest. Their curiosity was whetted, so they changed direction and walked across to investigate.

What they found was a group of good humoured, young people who were preparing a barbecue on the fringe of the beach. They had not heard the approach of Brian and Lucinda and looked up in surprise at their suddenly materializing among them.

'Why, hi there!' said a pert girl with red hair and freckles.

'We didn't mean to disturb you,' Lucinda apologized.

'No sweat! Say, that's a fine, old fashioned English accent,' grinned the redhead.

'I suppose that's because I am a fine, old fashioned, English girl,' Lucinda answered.

The rest of the group made them welcome and before they realized what had happened, they had been invited to join the barbecue. They ate, drank and chatted. Conversation was easy and time passed quickly. It was quite dark when the participants of the picnic packed up their things and departed for the beach house where they were staying. They asked Brian and Lucinda to come back with them for a good night drink but they declined. The light breeze which had sprung up at sunset had subsided and the air was still, warm and fragrant with the scent of the pine trees. They felt that this was a time when they wanted to be on their own, a private time, so they bade farewell to their convivial companions.

The moon had risen and the water was an iridescent silver as the waves sparkled against the pale sand. Stars shone from the black velvet sky and there was a hush all around them, broken only by the soft sighing of the sea. The night was pure magic and they were in its spell as they walked silently, arm in arm.

Brian halted and drew Lucinda to him. She turned her

face towards him and they kissed long and tenderly. Lucinda looked up at Brian's face, fine featured and shining in the moonlight and she felt desire rising within her. He was handsome and loving; the night was beautiful, the place perfect. Love was in the air. Moments of such complete enchantment do not come very often in a lifetime and, clasped in each other's arms, they gloried in the wonders of their bodies.

Lucinda ran her hands over the firm flesh of Brian's chest and her fingers tingled as he seemed to glow beneath her touch. He was stroking her hair, each caress an entreaty for her love. Looking into his adoring eyes, Lucinda was aware of her own loveliness and how it commanded homage from the young man's bewitched senses.

They found a shallow hollow among the dunes where the tall trees formed a curtain before which they enacted the age old ritual, the drama of man and woman.

Lucinda's fingers seemed to have a will of their own, finding all the hidden parts of his body, effortlessly sliding down his zip and opening him up to the restless seeking of her hands. He was big, smooth, impatient to enter and take her. Her nostrils caught the tang of his body, strongly male and, like his arms, it seemed to both encompass and comfort her. She wanted him, she wanted it, wildly and desperately, her whole body swollen by desire. She wriggled free of her panties and knew that she was gushing wet for her man.

Another time they would have played with each other, teasing and tantalizing, enticing and stimulating, before coming together. On this night, their desires were so heightened that such games were not only unnecessary: they would have made a mockery of their passion.

Lucinda sought a passage with her tongue between

Brian's lips and he drank in the honey of her breath. As her legs parted, she felt his weight, pressing down on her and she groaned with pleasure as he penetrated her. Her muscles tightened and she held him within her, possessing him as she was herself possessed. They lay, locked together, beneath the cold gaze of the moon and the stars, while time ceased and the earth moved to the rhythm of their bodies, rising and falling as the blood pounded in their veins. They were no longer two people but had become one being, inflamed by the one urge, their lips joined, their fingers intertwined, their hips and thighs united as they fused together until they exploded in one majestic orgasm which transfigured the night into a shimmering fantasy of which they were the sentient heart. Lucinda sank back in Brian's arms, her pulse still throbbing, light headed and exhausted as if she had just that moment awakened from a dream of such wild intensity that it had totally drained her.

After another eternity had passed, Brian eased away from her and mopped his drenched body.

'I wonder if there is another ferry back to the mainland or whether we shall have to spend the night on the beach,' he said.

'Does it matter?' Lucinda asked. Her body was heavy with fulfilment and everything else seemed to be trivial and irrelevant.

Brian waited for her mood to change. There was now a chill in the air and Lucinda gave a tiny shiver. She shook her head wearily and gave a quiet sigh.

'Let's go,' she said with the resignation of a child who knows that she has to quit the wonderful world of make believe and return to the reality of grown ups.

The last ferry had long departed but they were in luck. At the landing stage, they found a couple with a small motor launch who were about to make the crossing and who offered them a lift. Back in Sayville, Lucinda let them into the house with the key which Ulysses had given her. Of her uncle, there was no trace. He had given up waiting for their return and had made himself a simple meal, cleared up and gone to bed. Passing his door, they heard his measured breathing. They crept into their own room, undressed silently and curled up in the big, old fashioned bedstead.

It was nearly midday when Ulysses put a call through to Paul's hostel.

'I can't stop now,' Paul told him. 'I have to go to a lesson. But I have spoken to my photographic friend and he has promised to let me have the prints at four this afternoon. Could you be here some time after that?'

'One of us will come by,' Ulysses assured him. 'I hope that you got some really sensational shots.'

'We'll soon know,' Paul rejoined. 'I did remember to take off the lens cover but, in the general excitement, I might have taken some memorable pictures of my thumb.'

Ulysses hung up with a growl. 'There's nothing for it now except to sit and wait patiently,' he informed Brian and Lucinda and proceeded to pace up and down like a caged ant-eater with a weak bladder.

'Why don't we drive into town now and wait?' asked Brian.

'The longer we stay out of any place where Herbie might spot us, the better,' Ulysses stated. 'I don't suppose that he has got a lead onto the hostel but that guy is dangerous and there is no point in taking unnecessary risks.'

'So what do you propose? Do we all steal into New York wearing masks, wigs and fancy dress?'

'No need to be facetious, Lucinda,' replied her uncle.

'And I certainly do not think that it is a good idea for all three of us to parade through the city. Herbie will be looking for me, that's for sure. So I propose to remain here while one of you two sneak in.'

'I'll go,' Brian volunteered.

Ulysses shook his head. 'Better if Lucinda drives in. She has been in New York before. That's right, isn't it?'

'Yes. Since Mummy's family live in the States, I have been there many times.'

'So she knows her way around better than you do and she can find her way back here without any problem.'

Lucinda nodded her agreement. Brian offered to accompany her but this irritated Lucinda.

'Christ, man, do you think that I am some poor, weak, little woman who needs a gallant escort? Ulysses is right. Only one of us needs to go and that one is me.'

Consequently, after a light lunch, Lucinda took the car and drove off, leaving the two men to count the minutes until her return.

Ulysses stared at his watch as if by sheer concentration, he could persuade time to pass more quickly. Brian was not particularly happy at Lucinda running off to meet Paul but he hid his misgivings and settled down in an armchair with a book.

'Four o'clock,' Ulysses muttered. 'She ought to be there by now.'

There was the sound of footsteps advancing along the path to the house. Brian looked at Ulysses in consternation.

'I thought that you said that nobody ever comes here?'

'Wait. It's probably somebody who has mistaken the house. They'll go away in a minute.'

But the steps came closer. Then, there was the sound of a key being inserted in the lock.

'Can it be Lucinda? Maybe she forgot something.'

'No, Brian. We would have heard the car.'

They sat, stiff and immobile, listening to the key moving to and fro in the lock until, with a click, it engaged and the door swung open.

Brian had no idea what to expect. He found himself gazing at a tall, middle aged woman. She was well dressed and carried her clothes with the assurance of one who is conscious of her own importance – the sort of woman who gets a table in a crowded restaurant when lesser mortals have to stand in line, who gets the only taxi outside a theatre and for whom hall porters hurry to throw open doors. In short, she was a woman who was born to command and Brian found the expression on her strong, patrician face, daunting.

Ulysses' reaction was quite different. He threw back his head and burst out laughing with pent up relief.

'Good God, Melanie,' he greeted his sister. 'You gave me a terrible turn!'

'Doubtless the working of a guilty conscience,' commented Viscountess Hamblewood acidly.

'Not at all. But what are you doing here?'

'That is precisely the question which I wanted to put to you. And,' with a toss of her head in the direction of Brian, 'who is this young man?'

'He is a friend of Lucinda. She is in town and should be back before too long.'

Ulysses adopted a tone of sweet reasonableness and beamed at his sister as if her presence afforded him unimaginable pleasure.

'Well, now that you are here, sit down: make yourself comfortable.' Ulysses waved at a well padded easy chair. 'Can I fix you a drink or after all those years living in England, would you prefer a cup of tea?'

Melanie was not appeased but she allowed herself to be shepherded into the chair and when Ulysses bustled out of the kitchen, bearing a pot of delicately scented jasmine tea with some plain, sweet biscuits, she thawed sufficiently to explain how she happened to descend on the secluded Sayville house.

'You may have heard that I have been engaged on a lecture tour throughout the States,' she pronounced majestically.

'A stroke of genius by somebody to invite you,' Ulysses interrupted.

Melanie acknowledged his tribute with a nod of her head and continued. 'From time to time, I would call Gerald to make sure that he was coping. You know Gerald, so you understand why that would be necessary. However, it was not always possible for me to keep in as close touch as I would have wished because of the difference in time between here and England and because of the long hours I would get tied up with the lectures, questions and discussions and so on.'

She looked around as if to challenge anybody to dissent: Ulysses favoured her with a sympathetic smile.

'It was a couple of days ago, after I had been virtually isolated in Idaho, deprived of human company, that I got into Chicago and read something in one of the gossip columns of a local newspaper.'

'Are there no human beings in Idaho?' Brian asked innocently.

Melanie regarded him with undisguised scorn.

'Young man,' she declared, in the authoritative tone of an experienced lecturer, enlightening the masses, 'if you are under the impression that homo sapiens has advanced into Idaho, it is obvious that you have never been there. The most civilized inhabitants of that state are the cattle.'

Having thus disposed of the Idaho problem, Melanie resumed her narrative.

'According to this newspaper, there was something definitely odd going on back at Hamblewood. It seemed that all sorts of undesirable people were visiting the house but the writer was not exactly explicit on what they were doing there.'

'He'd probably had a couple of cups of Ero Tea or a brace of Sarah's Stiff Cock-tails,' Brian whispered to Ulysses.

'I wasn't really alarmed: I know the way the press likes to create sensations out of nothing, especially about British aristocrats, but I made a point of calling Gerald and demanding an explanation.' Melanie's features hardened. 'I couldn't make head or tail out of the nonsense he spouted.'

'What did he say?' Ulysses asked.

'Something about that I shouldn't worry, that there was a lot of money in sex and that the weather had been excellent. I got the feeling that he was hiding something and then he said that you, Ulysses, had been at Hamblewood. That was when I realized that there must be trouble.'

'That's most unjust.' Ulysses sounded hurt. 'Why, I was just passing through the UK.'

'Did anybody inform Scotland Yard?' Melanie enquired. 'Brother Ulysses, for as long as I can remember, you have meant trouble. Didn't you get thrown out of Princeton for selling the entire staff from the President down, shares in a non-existent gold mine in Brazil?'

'I let them have the shares at a discount,' Ulysses protested. 'Anyway, the mine was supposed to be in Uruguay. But I promise you, my business in Britain was strictly legitimate.'

'Indeed. Then perhaps you can cast some light on Gerald's babbling. What's all this about selling sex and, above all, what are you doing with him?'

'Why, sure,' Ulysses radiated honesty and nobody observing him could have had any inkling of how his agile mind was racing to invent a yarn sufficiently credible to convince his formidable sister. 'You know how your husband is an expert on cows and pigs and that sort of thing.'

'Gerald is not an expert on anything,' Melanie corrected Ulysses severely. 'But it is true that the welfare of the livestock is about the only thing at Hamblewood which occupies his time.'

'That's it,' agreed Ulysses. 'You see, he had run across this American and arranged to sell him some pigs – Herefords.'

'Herefords are cows,' Melanie intoned 'And what the hell has that to do with sex?'

'Sure, cows,' Ulysses amended hastily. 'Did I say pigs? A mere slip of the tongue. And as for sex, that was the whole point.'

'You are making as little sense as Gerald,' Melanie said.

'Not at all. It was all a matter of sex. You see, the American had wanted bulls and Gerald had shipped him cows. Wrong sex. As I was on my way to the States, I offered to clear the matter up for him. You know, arrange a new shipment and deal with the paper work.'

Ulysses smiled happily at Melanie.

'Have another cup of tea,' he proffered, as if that would make his story more convincing.

'Rubbish!' Melanie thundered. 'Nobody could be that stupid.'

'We are talking about Gerald,' Ulysses reminded her timidly.

Melanie's expression became thoughtful. She nodded slowly and her face clouded over.

'You're right. There is one man who could be that stupid without any effort. So that is what all the fuss is about?'

'Would I lie to you?' Ulysses pleaded.

'Don't push me too hard,' Melanie retorted.

'What I don't understand,' Brian interposed, 'is how you knew that you would find your brother here, Lady Hamblewood.'

'Oh, that's no mystery. He and I were the only people to know of the place after the death of my father. Whenever Ulysses was up to some skulduggery, he would always hide out here. And that's a point, Ulysses. If you are here on legitimate business, why are you holed up here as if you had a difference of opinion with a Mafia boss? Won't the decent hotels accept you in New York City?'

'Jesus, you are suspicious. As a matter of fact, we have been staying in one of the most pretentious hotels until yesterday. The kids wanted a break, so I thought of taking them away for a couple of days. Here, they are close to the ocean; they can swim, take the sun – '

'Yes, I get the picture,' Melanie interrupted. 'Don't get too elaborate, brother, the simpler your stories, the better I like them.'

'Do have another cup of tea,' Ulysses begged.

Melanie relented. She accepted the tea and she and her long lost brother began to chat about old times and forgotten friends. After about half an hour of small talk, their original tension had vanished. Ulysses was charming: Melanie was amused. Brian witnessed this transformation and his respect for the cunning of Ulysses grew mightily. All was sweetness and light.

At last, Melanie got to her feet.

'I must be on my way,' she announced.

'Oh, what a pity! Can't you stay a bit longer until Lucinda gets back? She will be sorry to miss you.'

'Ulysses, I am in a good mood. Why spoil it by confronting me with my daughter? No, seriously, I have to get back for a meeting which I am due to address tonight. I am the main after dinner speaker,' she told them with some pride.

So after prolonged farewells, Melanie left. Her parting words to her brother were:

'Now, Ulysses, I am relying on you. Please, do take care of Gerald and of Lucinda too. They both are experts in getting into trouble and I can't be there to dig them out. You have the Blake brains – and enough experience in getting out of sticky situations for the whole family.'

'I assure you that I shall watch over them night and day,' Ulysses said solemnly.

'And do come back to Hamblewood when I am there. We ought not to drift apart: the Blakes should stick together. And as for you, young man,' she inclined her head towards Brian. 'It has been a pleasure meeting you.'

With that, she was gone.

Brian stared at Ulysses in open admiration.

'How did you manage it? Talk about the Taming of the Shrew!'

'I'll let you into a secret, dear boy. Just a tiniest spot of that nectar, no more than a drop or two, has a wonderfully soothing influence.'

'The tea?'

'The tea.'

'Thank God, you didn't give her an overdose!'

At about the same time that Viscountess Hamblewood had tracked down her brother, Lucinda was knocking at the door of Paul's room. He half opened the door, saw who it was and ushered her into the room.

'I have only this minute got back with the prints,' he said. 'You might like to cast your eye over them and give me your opinion.'

Lucinda perched on his bed and Paul sat down beside her. He handed her an envelope from which she took about twenty photographs. She studied them carefully and whistled softly.

'Gee,' she breathed, 'talk about geriatric gymnastics!'

'I thought that we might publish them under the title, Sex for Senior Citizens,' Paul suggested.

'Do they turn you on?' Paul asked as Lucinda concentrated on the pictures.

'No, not at all,' she answered. 'They're simply too weird. I have my kinky moments,' she told him with a smile, 'but at heart, I am a hopeless romantic.'

'This is more in your line.'

Paul walked over to an upright piano which stood open against the wall. The instrument was by no means new, rather shabby and slightly battered, but it was a good make, in tune and in good internal condition. Some music was on the rest: Paul had clearly been practising recently but he ignored the notes in front of him as he sat at the piano and started to play.

Lucinda had been impressed when she heard Paul perform at The Black Cockatoo but she was surprised at the change in his style. She had a vague recollection of the music he was playing and had an idea that it was one of the less frequently heard Chopin nocturnes. The melody hung in the air like a string of moonbeams above chords of chromatic anguish. Never before had she heard so eloquent an avowal of the bliss and the agony of love. Behind the rise and fall of the wordless song, the music spoke of a longing of such intensity that she felt the tears springing to her eyes. Paul's long, sensitive fingers coaxed the passion out of the wooden keys as if, by his touch, he was endowing them with a life of their own.

As the last note died away, there was a magic which persisted, filling the bare room and possessing both of them. Without a word, Lucinda walked over and kissed Paul, softly and tenderly. He half turned in his seat and laid his hand on her wrist, his touch both caressing and beseeching her.

'Play some more,' she murmured, her voice husky with emotion.

'Later,' he whispered.

Not another word was spoken. The music had brought them into perfect harmony and had quickened their desire to such a pitch that mere language would have been a defilement of their exaltation. Paul folded her in his arms and with a sigh of contentment, she let herself sink into his long embrace.

They made love on his single student's bed, oblivious to the discomfort and the cramp. They came together so naturally, without any strain or effort, it was as if they were two halves of a being which had been seeking all their lives to achieve this inevitable reunion. Paul's hands stroked her breasts which nestled beneath his touch so snugly that she knew that this was where they belonged. Lucinda was fascinated by the contrast of his dark skin against her fair flesh. She took his hand in hers and guided it slowly from her chest towards her belly.

Soon after, he lowered himself between her legs and began kissing and caressing her bellybutton. At first it tickled a bit, but then she could hardly wait to feel his big full lips embrace her clitoris, which was by now, swollen and throbbing with desire. He teased her, climbed on top of her again and kissed her on the nose and mouth, while his strong arms lifted her up by the buttocks. His tremendous cock tantalized her hips, thighs and belly and came dangerously close to penetrating her eager pussy.

As she looked between their bellies she noted once more the glistening purple mushroom head that sprouted at the end of his brown shaft. She had seldom been so horny for any man in her life and she almost forced him inside her own body, virtually begging him to stop teasing her and get on with what she wanted most at this moment: to get fucked by this black beauty with his ever so velvety skin and bedroom eyes.

Her long slender legs fitted against his powerful limbs and he moved inside her as if they had always been united, one passion within one flesh and what rhythm. . .

Lucinda ran her fingers through Paul's crisp, curly hair: it was like a tiny electric shock, making her flesh tingle. There was something about him which made him different from any other man she had ever known, a unique combination of strength and softness. His cock was big and firm. As it pierced and held her, she submitted to its power, yet its strokes, like every other aspect of Paul's love-making, had a sensitivity, almost a delicacy which charmed rather than compelled.

There was a joy in the play of their bodies, a physical fulfilment of the restless questing of the Chopin nocturne which still echoed in her ears and which had triggered her will to join her body to that of the man who, at that moment, encompassed the whole world for her.

And Paul worshipped her with all his body. He loved her and he fucked her without any need for sexual athletics or adolescent artifices. He was simple and direct but Lucinda was conscious of his burning sincerity and her body thrilled to his warmth. Their climax was sweet, yet it brought no cloying, no after-taste of sorrow or regret, just the peace of something that was perfect in itself.

If only she could have laid there all day beside him, free from all outside worries and stress. But she recalled Ulysses, waiting in the house at Sayville, impatient to know how his ruse against Hiram and Semiramide had worked out. Reluctantly she raised herself on one elbow, gazed down into the face of her lover, and gave him a parting kiss.

'Do you have to go so soon?'

'You know they will be waiting for me. I ought to have left before.'

'But you will come back? What I mean is we shall do this again? It wasn't simply a passing whim – over and done with.'

'You know it wasn't.' Lucinda regarded him, somehow both proud and pleading. 'I don't think that I could bear to leave you like that. We hardly know each other, but this is sort of special, isn't it?'

By way of answer, he kissed her, his doubts dispelled.

'Off you go, then. Back to the other men who need you.' His tone was jocular but tinged with regret, and perhaps even a trace of envy.

Lucinda quickly fixed her face, grabbed the envelope and hurried out. As she left, she heard Paul start to play again. She recognized Liszt's 'Liebestraum'. Love's dream, she said to herself, as she ran to where the car was parked.

She found her way out of the city without difficulty. As she drove, she reflected on her conduct. It would not be true to say that she felt guilty at having slept with Paul only hours after that idyllic night on the beach with Brian. She did not belong to either man and she had never promised her undivided affection to anybody. Yet, she was startled that she could feel so deeply for them both and turn from one to the other so abruptly. It must have been the music, she assured herself, but she did not believe it was as straightforward as that. She wondered whether her emotions were so facile, was she simply a shallow bitch? No, it wasn't guilt that she experienced, but it was a feeling remarkably like it.

As she approached Sayville, Lucinda collected herself. She could deal with her own emotions at her leisure. In a minute, she would have to face Brian and the last thing she wanted was to revive his jealousy. She determined to put on a bold front. She swung off the road and left the car on the apron in the front of the garage. With a jaunty step, she went up the short path and let herself into the house.

'Dirty pictures!' she called. 'Absolutely filthy pictures! Who will buy my disgusting studies, all delivered in plain brown envelopes? Guaranteed shocking, amazing, astounding!'

She waved her trophy encouragingly.

Her uncle's reaction was not what she had expected. He looked meaningfully at Brian and said with heart-felt relief,

'Thank God she didn't come in with that damned fool display five minutes earlier. Just think of the effect she would have had on her mother.'

He shuddered. And only then did he seize the envelope and examine its contents.

CHAPTER 11

Brian recounted to Lucinda the confrontation of her uncle, the wiliest of the Blakes, by her mother, the most forceful of the clan. The news was a shock but Lucinda survived and congratulated herself on her escape.

Meanwhile Ulysses had examined carefully the photographs and expressed his satisfaction with them.

'So, what's our next move?' Lucinda asked.

'The next move is mine, not ours,' Ulysses corrected her. 'The time has come for the hateful Herbie to be faced with the evidence of his misdeeds.'

'You mean that you are going to blackmail him with those pictures?'

'What an indelicate way you have of putting things,' her uncle commented. 'But, you saw what a gaggle of wealthy clients he had assembled in his home of rest. I don't think that he would want to lose such lucrative loonies, do you?'

'That's what I said,' Lucinda chuckled happily, 'blackmail.'

Ulysses sighed and abandoned his efforts to distil a sense of diplomacy into his niece. 'Excuse me,' he said, 'I have an important call to make.'

There followed a protracted and informative conversation between Ulysses and the telephone operator as he went through Hiram's impressive list of aliases until the operator came up with a number where that man of many personalities could be located. Brian and Lucinda listened attentively to the Sayville half of the ensuing conversation.

'Hello, Herbie, I am sure that you know who's speaking.'

There was a pause: Ulysses wrinkled up his nose and shook his head sadly.

'Tut tut, that is not the sort of language I would expect from a man of your talents. You should wash your mouth out with soap and water.'

There was a faint spluttering over the phone which was clearly audible throughout the room. When it had subsided, Ulysses continued.

'It seems to me that it could be to the advantage of both of us if we were to meet and resume our conversation which was so comically interrupted yesterday.'

Ulysses listened to Hiram's reply and then said testily,

'Of course I am serious. Why else should I bother to track you down and call you? I have something to show you which I am sure that you will find of absorbing interest. Now, you listen. I shall see you tomorrow, but alone, understand? None of your pet gorillas. Where am I? Well, I think that is a piece of information which I shall keep to myself, at least for the present. Do you remember that bar we used to patronise on Second Avenue between Forty-fourth and Forty-fifth? What did you say? The sordid place run by a couple of filthy fags – that's it, I couldn't have put it more delicately. Well now, you be there at six tomorrow, and make sure that you are alone. Got that? Fine.'

He slammed down the phone although Hiram was still talking and beamed benevolently at the others.

'We'll go with you,' said Brian.

'You most certainly won't. You heard me insist that Herbie comes alone. It goes without saying that so do I.'

'But do you trust him?'

'It's because I don't trust him, Lucinda, that I have

made it a condition that we meet in a bar where there are always plenty of people about at that time of day.'

'Even so. Lucinda was plainly unhappy.

'I assure you that I shall be much safer without you than if you were to accompany me. Think, girl. I'll take those prints and show them to Herbie. I shall make it clear that the negatives are in your possession and that if anything unpleasant were to happen to me, you have received instructions on how to use them. You may have noticed that Paul got one last admirable picture which quite clearly shows Herbie himself in the middle of the Bacchanalia. So while I carry on our negotiations, you will stay hidden and look after those negatives.'

'And me?' demanded Brian.

'You stay well away and look after Lucinda. Now, that's quite enough. There's nothing more to be done until tomorrow, so let's enjoy ourselves.'

They went out for a meal. Ulysses chirruped away merrily enough but Lucinda was subdued and Brian watched her thoughtfully. Conversation became more and more desultory and Ulysses was quite relieved when they decided unanimously on having an early night and he was rid of his moody companions.

Back in their bedroom, Lucinda undressed quickly and slipped into bed. Brian watched her in silence, feeling the tension which had grown up.

Lucinda feigned a yawn. 'Do hurry up, darling. I'm absolutely bushed: do you mind if we go straight to sleep?'

Brian stalked off into the bathroom without answering and when he got back, Lucinda's eyes were firmly closed, she lay still and her breathing was slow and regular. Brian was not deceived.

'You fucked him, didn't you.' He was not asking but

accusing her, making a bald statement in a flat, deliberate tone in which resentment was mingled with disgust.

'Mm, what?' Lucinda murmured dreamily.

'You're a lousy actress. I'm sure that you've had a busy day, but you are still wide awake.'

Lucinda's brain was in a turmoil. She did not want to hurt Brian but she was emotionally with Paul: the impression of that afternoon remained with her and she was not yet ready to switch her attention back to Brian. She knew that he would not understand but she had not the heart to lie to him. So she remained silent.

'How could you, Lucinda?' Brian demanded bitterly. 'Wasn't last night good enough or can't you stay faithful for more than one day?'

At once, her pity for him and her sense of having been unfair to him gave way to annoyance.

'What are you talking about?' she flared up. 'Faithful? Have I ever made you any promise which gives you some sort of claim on me?'

'Some promises can be made without words.'

'Stop talking romantic rubbish.'

'Was last night, making love on the beach in the moonlight, romantic rubbish?'

'No, it was marvellous,' Lucinda's voice was gentler. 'I enjoy being with you, Brian, and when we make love, it is heavenly. But, can't you understand that my body is my own and if I go to bed with somebody else, that does not mean that I've gone off you?'

'You're a promiscuous bitch,' he replied.

'All right, if that is how you want to think of me,' she said with an air of resignation.

'How else can I think of you? Are you in love with this Paul?'

Lucinda considered. 'I don't honestly know. Perhaps,

but I don't think so. But how can I get you to realize that even if I am in love with him or anyone else, it doesn't alter my feelings for you?'

Brian lay still and quiet in the bed. Lucinda could feel his misery and she moved over to touch him. He recoiled away from her.

'Please, the last thing I feel like is a mercy fuck.'

'Damn you, Brian, I only wanted to give you a hug. I can't go to sleep with this wall of mistrust between us.'

He laughed sardonically. 'A sisterly embrace?'

Beneath his anger and hurt pride, Lucinda knew that he needed to be comforted and she desired to give that comfort. She put her arms around him and she felt him stiffen against her and then relax. The warmth and the scent of his body were seductive, but she knew that this was not the moment to surrender to her innate horniness.

'Let's not fight,' she whispered. 'We've been over this time and time again. You know the sort of person I am. Can't we enjoy our own relationship without bothering about what goes on with other people? I don't have any claim on you.'

'I don't want any other woman,' Brian confessed.

'You will. It'll happen to you some day and I promise you that I shall understand and I won't be any less loving. Please, Brian, don't be jealous.'

He was not happy but he was rather more reconciled. He put his arms around her and squeezed her tenderly in tacit assent.

'We'd better get some sleep,' he told her. 'If your uncle is going to confront Hiram tomorrow, we might find ourselves in for a busy time.'

Lucinda kissed him. 'Goodnight, darling.'

They lay close together and Brian was aware of the consolation of her body, feline and sexy, nestling around him but it was a long time before he had recovered his composure sufficiently to fall asleep. As for Lucinda, she felt torn between her affection for Brian and her newly awakened sensual passion for Paul. For all her brave words, she feared that there would be difficult times ahead for them.

The next day dragged interminably until it was time for Ulysses to depart for his meeting. Brian tried to persuade him to reconsider and let at least one of them go with him but Ulysses was adamant.

Daley's Bar was not an architectural gem and it was unlikely to attract tourists who desired closer acquaintance with New York's cultural heritage. Nevertheless, as Ulysses had reckoned, by the time he arrived, the place was thronged with its habitual clientele of men and women who worked or lived nearby, passing taxi drivers, salesmen, con artists, professional Irishmen, serious drinkers and, reassuringly, even a couple of cops who were checking that all was well. For Daley's Bar had been the scene of some monumental fights and Ulysses had known that it was under constant surveillance by the forces of law and order.

Around the bar, there was much noise and confusion as Daley himself, in shirt sleeves, dispensed Guinness. The lighting was dim but was sufficient to reveal the finely developed patina of grime, overlaid with dust, which distinguished the decor. Benches lined the walls except for where there stood a juke box and a trio of bleeping and clattering electronic games, the machines adding a touch of modernity which seemed out of place. At the low tables in the middle of the bar sat moody, solitary drinkers or more animated groups who had graduated from Guinness to Irish whiskey. A few highly painted ladies were attempting to wean some of the men away from drink to a form of physical activity which would involve dollars passing from the men to the women. In that milieu, they were not meeting with much success.

Ulysses pushed his way through the crowd and almost immediately saw Hiram, sitting at one of the tables. He was not alone. Semiramide was beside him, busily demolishing a gin and tonic. Ulysses approached warily and took a seat opposite the two of them.

'I told you that you should be alone,' he said. Hiram looked amused and shrugged his shoulders.

'I didn't think that you would object to your old flame. You can see that I haven't brought any heavies and Frankie isn't really a person: she's just my shadow.'

Ulysses grunted and the lady in question glared at him.

'O.K. She can stay.'

'So, what do you want?' Hiram's eyes were as watchful as a hawk's but Ulysses gave him a friendly smile.

'Relax, Herbie. You and I are going to do a spot of trading.'

'I wish you would stop calling me Herbie. I am Hiram. These flashes from the past are merely confusing.'

'Anything for a pal. Well, Herbie-now-Hiram, let's get down to business.'

'And what have I got that you want?' asked Hiram.

'Money.'

'That figures,' Hiram admitted. 'But what have you got that could possibly be of interest to me?'

Ulysses smiled grimly. 'I would say that your Deare Center is a highly profitable operation. Now, I am a great believer in old-fashioned American enterprise and if you rake in the dollars because a batch of idiots are prepared to part with their money in order to have their non-existent illnesses treated by your white coated nursing thugs, that's fine with me. But, what do you think will be the reaction of your clients if these pictures are published in the national press?'

Ulysses tossed the envelope containing the photographs onto the table: Hiram picked it up and he and Semiramide studied the contents.

Semiramide immediately voiced her opinion of Ulysses.

'You low-down, filthy, snivelling bastard!'

'You know me so well,' Ulysses replied humbly. 'But what do you think, Hiram? Of course, I am asking your view of the publicity value of the pictures not their quality as works of art.'

Hiram was concentrating on the exhibits and slowly, a broad smile spread across his face.

'Well, I do congratulate you,' he beamed at Ulysses. 'They really have captured the spirit of the thing. And this is what you want to sell me?'

'Obviously I have the negatives stashed away which I will make available to you once we have a deal.'

Hiram burst out laughing. 'Why, you crazy nut, what makes you think that I would pay to suppress these pictures?'

Ulysses looked disappointed. 'Being insulted by Frankie is to be expected but I had thought that you had better manners, Herbie.'

'Hiram,' corrected his adversary. Then his tone became more earnest. 'Think for a minute, man. You've seen the sort of people we have at the Center. The biggest group are rich, old broads whose husbands will pay virtually anything to have them taken off their hands. And most of these respectable ladies haven't been decently laid for more years than they can remember. What do you think happened after you and your accomplices left the clinic? Do you think, once the effect of your drug wore off, that the old girls were outraged? Not on your life, pal! They wanted to know when the next session would be taking place. If the word gets out that regular orgies are staged at the Deare Center, we shall be overwhelmed by applications for admission from every sex-starved woman in the state and have you any concept of how many that would be? No, Ulysses, if you want to do me a favour, don't suppress those pictures, have them printed in every newspaper in the country.'

Ulysses stared at him in dismay.

'You know,' he said slowly, 'that was not the reaction which I had anticipated. And how much would you pay me to distribute them?'

Hiram chuckled, 'A hell of a lot less than you were going to ask for having them destroyed.'

The two men regarded each other silently. Ulysses was trying to assess the likelihood that Hiram was bluffing. Semiramide's contribution was to request Hiram in lurid terms to carry out fantastic atrocities on the person of Ulysses. As if to resolve Ulysses' doubts, Hiram made another point.

'You said that I have money. That's right. Now, you ought to remember what life is like in New York. Listen, punk, I can buy whatever and whoever I want in this city. Newspaper editors, police chiefs, even the undertakers, they all get a pay off. So just what do you hope to pull?'

Ulysses got to his feet. 'I guess that I shall have to try and find some other merchandise more to your taste.'

He started to walk out, but Hiram took him by the arm.

'Now, don't be so hasty. Your art products are of no value. But there is something else which you have which does interest me.'

Ulysses stared at him thoughtfully.

'And what precisely have you in mind?'

'You know well enough. That stuff you gave the

inmates is dynamite. When Frankie first told me how it had affected her, I thought that she was exaggerating or just finding an excuse for her endless horniness.'

Semiramide started to protest, but Hiram silenced her and continued.

'Now I have seen what it does. So, how about it, Ulysses? How much do you want for the formula?'

Ulysses shook his head. 'No way. The formula is not for sale.'

'Now, be reasonable.' Hiram's tone was friendly, but there was a hard glint in his eyes which contradicted his apparent affability. 'I just told you, I have friends here. I don't know where you are hiding out but within twenty-four hours I can find out and something regrettable might happen to you – or to your friends. Do you read me, Ulysses?'

'Now who is being hasty?' Ulysses countered. 'I said that the formula is not for sale. I am prepared to do a deal on supplying the stuff.'

Hiram considered and then asked:

'Are you able to give me sole rights to market your love-juice in New York city?'

'I can do better than that. Tell me, how big an area could you handle?'

Hiram laughed. 'I have the contacts to take the whole country.'

'Fine. The United States are yours.'

Ulysses pulled up a chair and sat down again at the table. He regarded Hiram with mild interest. Hiram's face was a study: greed lured him on, doubt and mistrust held him back. As ever, Semiramide was ready with practical advice.

'Honey, you are not thinking of doing a deal with that sneaky snake?' she shouted.

Hiram dismissed her with an impatient toss of his head.

'Quiet! Business is too important a matter for dames – it says so in the Bible or somewhere.'

'You're crazy!'

Semiramide's objections were cut short by Hiram who slapped her sharply on the cheek. Ulysses looked amused: nobody else in the bar took any notice; it was that sort of bar.

'The whole country could be my territory?' Hiram reiterated. 'And how much would you be expecting me to pay? I don't even know how you deliver the stuff: is it by the ounce or by the ton?'

'Oh, I assure you that a very little goes a long way. But, you know, this has never been marketed before so there is no price on the street which we can use.' Ulysses considered the problem for a moment and then went on, 'What I propose is that I send you a trial shipment and you pay me something on account. That will give you a chance to see what you can get for the stuff and to estimate how much of it you can take. Then we can work out a fair price. How does that strike you.'

'It sounds all right,' Hiram answered, 'but let's get down to specifics. How much cold cash are you asking?'

'One long one.'

'A million bucks? Without having received any merchandise, you must be crazy.'

'Steady, Hiram, think of your blood pressure. I am willing to ship in the consignment first and you pay me only when I hand it over.'

'That's better.' Hiram was partly mollified. 'But a million, that's one hell of a lot of money. And how big is this trial shipment going to be?'

'If you think of what I gave your fair companion,' Ulysses gave a friendly nod at Semiramide who scowled back at him, 'as one fix, you'll get enough for about ten thousand.'

'Why, that won't be sufficient for me to get my investment back,' complained Hiram.

'That depends on how you sell it,' Ulysses told him complacently. 'You know as well as I do that you will be able to charge what you like. Anyway, I have certain expenses to cover, so I am not prepared to take one cent less. And, don't forget, if you are happy with the quality, once the channels are established, I can send you in really big shipments – as much as you can handle. And you will have the exclusive rights in the States. I'll tell you what. I'm feeling generous, so I'll throw in Canada as a bonus.'

'Still, a million,' Hiram demurred.

'A million, take it or leave it. And payable in nice laundered money from your Swiss bank account to my Swiss bank account. Understood?'

'You are a tough customer,' Hiram commented. 'And how do you know that I have a Swiss account?'

Ulysses snapped his fingers in a gesture of impatience.

'Quit stalling! Have we a deal?'

Hiram grinned. 'Yes, my dear old friend, we are in business. That is, provided you can deliver as you say. How long will it take you?'

Ulysses took a few seconds to consider.

'Give me ten days. I'll call you at your asylum. And make sure that you have the money ready: I don't give credit.'

Ulysses got up, bestowed a smile of undiluted venom on Semiramide and took his leave.

As soon as he had passed through the door, Semiramide turned on Hiram.

'How can you be so stupid as to do a deal with that crook?' she demanded angrily.

'Calm down,' Hiram smirked, 'do you think that Ulysses is the only one capable of a little cheating?'

'Oh, I get it.' Semiramide's countenance cleared. 'When he brings in the dope, we hit him.'

'Something along those lines,' Hiram agreed.

'Good. I feel better now.' Semiramide's eyes shone and she ordered another large gin and tonic.

When he got back to Sayville, Ulysses told the others what had transpired.

'Thank heaven you are safe,' Lucinda exclaimed. 'I was worried rigid about you, alone with that couple of brigands.'

But Brian had been thinking and his conclusion was much the same as Semiramide's.

'Once you have the nectar here, won't Hiram simply seize it and dispose of you in some unpleasant manner?'

'The suspicion had crossed my mind,' Ulysses conceded, 'but, if I play my cards right, there should be no risk. As long as he does not know where the nectar comes from, he won't want to eliminate me. After all, he knows that this first shipment is a small one and he will be eager to get his hands on a bulk supply.'

'So, won't he be watching you to see where you bring in the heather?' asked Lucinda.

'You can be sure that from now on, I won't be able to turn over in bed without it being reported to Hiram. And we had better get down to planning our moves carefully so that he stays in his present delicious state of innocence.'

CHAPTER 12

'A gentleman always removes his socks before getting into bed with a lady,' Semiramide informed Hiram. 'It is laid down in all the best books on good manners and what they call etiquette.'

'What about if a gentleman gets into bed with some female who ain't no lady?' he retorted.

'Ulysses took off his socks,' Semiramide observed smugly.

They were in Semiramide's garishly overfurnished penthouse, so recently the scene of her seduction by Ulysses and a stiff dose of heather nectar. Hiram had just indulged in his own brand of foreplay. This consisted of removing the bare minimum of his garments and announcing that he wanted to get laid. That was all and Semiramide had felt justifiably that the proposition lacked romance. In a word, she was not turned on.

'Aren't you going to do anything to get me warmed up?' she complained.

'That's the reason for the socks,' Hiram explained triumphantly. 'I would never ask you to fuck with cold feet, not like that fink, Ulysses.'

'Why do I put up with a slob like you?' Semiramide mused, as she began to undress.

'Because I am the guy who keeps you in the manner to which you have now become accustomed. Hurry up, as soon as we have finished I want to take a shower.'

'You great baboon, you ought to take your shower before you get into my bed.'

'That is my normal practice: I make an exception in your case.'

'Bastard!'

Such were the preliminaries to their sexual encounter. In some perverse way, Hiram's very cruddiness did appeal to Semiramide. He could put on the act of being a civilized person but, on those occasions, she had the sensation that he was indeed playing a part, the con man off duty. His vulgarity came naturally to him and so she got the impression of a sincerity in his pretty basic love-making. Also, it must be admitted, she was not the most refined of women so they were actually a well matched couple, once they got going.

She climbed into the bed, swinging her ample haunches enticingly. Hiram grabbed her and gave her an appreciative pinch.

'Your upholstery is still in good shape,' he told her. 'I like a woman with something to get hold of.'

Her reaction was to find the obvious part of his anatomy for her to get hold of.

'Holy Christ, go easy!' he hollered. 'That's fragile.'

Semiramide's response was to squeeze harder.

'O.K., Hiram baby, are you going to act nice and loving? Or do you want me to pull it right off.'

Faced with those alternatives, Hiram's attitude underwent a sudden and drastic alteration.

'Now, nice and gentle,' she commanded, 'nibble my ear!'

Hiram complied. Semiramide closed her eyes. She had always been susceptible to this treatment. A delicious tremor ran through her body and she uttered a low moan. Her grasp relaxed and Hiram, liberated but chastened, continued to pay his respects to her ear while sliding sensually between Semiramide's legs and forcing his way into her passive, unresisting body.

Semiramide kept her eyes tight shut and clasped his powerful, stocky body in her arms.

'Push your tongue right in!' she told him, her voice sunk to a faint whisper.

In her imagination Semiramide was no longer with her prosaic bedmate, but back more years than she cared to reckon with the man who had first sucked and probed her ear and unlocked those mental restraints of which she had been unaware, but which had until then, denied her the joy of complete, wild abandon. His name was Roberto, the son of an Italian immigrant, a mere boy, with long, silky hair and eyes as black as coal. He was not her first lover: she had started young, but her earliest adventures had been with youths who knew nothing about a woman's sexuality and who were actuated by curiosity rather than lust. They were no more than groping encounters, clumsy and eventually unsatisfying, nearly as sordid as Hiram's essays in wooing. But Roberto was different. She closed her eyes more tightly and it was his fingers which were roaming over her flesh. It was for him that her nipples were straining and her juices flowing uncontrollably. Once more, she was in her teens – fresh, sweet and desirable. Her skin was smooth and firm and Roberto was madly in love with her. His breath was as fragrant as honeysuckle and her blood raced just at the sight of him. And his smile, radiant as sunshine – he was so young and yet so wonderfully mature and knowing in the lore of love and the needs of a woman. She could hear his panting as his fine, thick shaft drove into her, faster and faster, harder and harder and, all the time, his tongue, long and agile, a second penis, was playing in her ear, making her writhe in a demonic dance of frenzied longing. His hands gripped her tight and she felt herself totally possessed. Roberto had become her life, all her senses drugged by the feel and the scent of him as, with her eyes closed, she yielded every cell of her own glorious body to his potent maleness, rushing towards her great, wild orgasm and, at the same time, spurring him on to his own, as much a slave to her animal desire as she was to his. It was coming: she could sense the change in his body and the growing excitement and anticipation of her own. Her heart was pounding as if to burst. His muscles were taut steel, binding her and she clung to him as if to hold him for ever, while he plunged deeper and deeper inside her. And then, she screamed as she lost herself in that magic moment of climax. She felt herself, quivering and quaking, completely out of control. There was one huge, final heave of his body and then he went limp. They collapsed, they died, they lay there, inert and motionless. Reluctantly, Semiramide opened her eyes and regarded Hiram, still puffing from his exertions, his paunch heaving.

'Well,' he said, his chest swelling with pride and self satisfaction, 'that was pretty good. Aren't I still the greatest stud you've ever had?'

She closed her eyes again and sighed for the past.

'Go and take your shower,' she said.

Hiram waddled off and was soon splashing away happily. Semiramide, in a reverie, visualized Roberto as he had been at their last meeting and then realized with a shock that he would by now be about the same age as Hiram and perhaps as unappetizing.

'I'd like to know what Ulysses is doing right now,' Hiram called from the bathroom.

'He said he would get in touch when he had the shipment ready,' Semiramide replied.

'I know that. But I would be much happier if I could keep him under observation before. Maybe we could get a lead on where he gets this stuff of his.'

Semiramide laughed pityingly, 'Ulysses is smart. He knows that you are as much to be trusted as a skunk's ass: he'll be making sure that he is invisible.'

'I guess that you are right but it won't do any harm to tell the boys to look out for him. You never know: we might just strike it lucky.'

Semiramide was wrong. Ulysses was busy, moving out of his secluded hide-out in Sayville and installing himself in a midtown hotel, right in the middle of the tourist and the business circuits. Brian and Lucinda moved into another and rather humbler establishment. They went about the city discreetly and did nothing to draw attention to themselves. The same cannot be said of Ulysses. He flitted from bar to bar, looked in at the trendiest discos, sex clubs, gyms, saunas and eating houses. There was not one 'in-place' in town where he was not ostentatiously in. Virtually within hours, his movements were being reported to a surprised but delighted Hiram.

Hiram expected that his quarry would go abroad to collect his mysterious merchandise and he arranged accordingly to have him shadowed. But days passed and Ulysses remained as attached as ever to the New York landscape. Semiramide ran into him one evening. He was affable and generous enough to take her to an expensive dinner. He chattered away throughout the meal until she turned to the subject that was nagging at her mind and that of Hiram.

'What am I doing about shipping in the goods,' he said, echoing her question. 'I have the matter under control. Do tell Hiram.'

'So, he must have an accomplice who is somewhere abroad, getting the stuff together,' Hiram concluded. 'We'll have to pick up the trail when it enters the country.'

The next evening, Ulysses was taking a quiet drink at

the bar of the Waldorf when Hiram slithered onto the next stool.

'Well, now, this is an unexpected pleasure. What would you like to drink?'

'Just a tomato juice,' Hiram said. 'I'm on a crash diet to lose some weight.'

'Good idea,' Ulysses gazed disapprovingly at Hiram's wandering waistline.

'Were you planning on meeting somebody?' asked Ulysses, as he sipped his large Scotch.

'No, no, just passing by,' Hiram answered. He hurriedly gulped down his tomato juice and mopped his brow. 'Gee, was I thirsty! Let's have another.'

'I haven't finished this yet,' Ulysses pointed out.

'No matter, you'll be able to manage.'

Hiram had already summoned a waiter and ordered the same again.

When a third double Scotch had been deposited by his elbow, Ulysses was frowning with displeasure. What offended his sense of propriety was not his opponent's ploy, but his lack of subtlety. However, he was quite prepared to play along. Silently, he thanked his Creator for giving him, in addition to a tongue of silver, a stomach of iron.

Hiram waited until Ulysses had consumed an appreciable quantity of the potent liquor before turning the conversation away from general topics.

'You haven't forgotten about our deal, have you, Ulysses, old pal?'

His tone was casual, but there was a wary glitter to his eye.

'Everything's going to plan,' Ulysses told him. He giggled happily, belched and blinked owlishly at his inquisitor.

'Say, Ulysses,' Hiram was all honeyed concern, 'you know, things aren't like they were in the old days.'

'Issat so?' Ulysses' speech was slurred and he shook his head in sympathy.

'Now, take your little problem, for example.'

'Problem? Have I got a problem?'

'Sure, you have a problem.' Hiram smiled in a kindly way at his Scotch soddened comrade. 'But, don't worry, I can help.'

'That's good of you.' Tears of gratitude welled up in Ulysses' eyes. 'You know, I didn't even know I had a problem until you told me and now, I won't give it another thought. Thank you, Herbie.'

'Hiram,' corrected his benefactor. 'But if I am going to sort things out for you, Ulysses, you must trust me. You do trust me, don't you?'

'Of course, I trust you! Didn't you just deal with my problem, old buddy?'

'Not yet,' Hiram explained, 'but, here we go. You see, Ulysses, you have to bring this drug, whatever it is, into the country. Correct?'

'Absolutely right. Couldn't have put it more clearly. You always did have a terrific grasp of things, even when you were Herbie, Hiram.'

So, we know that it has not been here all the time, thought Hiram. We're beginning to make progress.

'Like I was telling you, things have changed. You used to be able to walk anything through the customs at any airport. Now, what with sniffer dogs, X-rays, lasers and God knows what else, you can't bring in a box of candy, without somebody stopping you and giving you a body search.'

'Shouldn't be allowed,' Ulysses proclaimed indignantly, 'you should complain to the President.'

'That's O.K.,' soothed Hiram. 'I have my friends. Now, if you let me know how and when you are bringing in this stuff, I'll get it eased through. You follow me?'

'You're a good sort, Hiram,' Ulysses patted his head as if he were an obedient dog which had brought his master his slippers. 'But you don't have to bother.'

'It's no sweat.'

'Remember, my sister married a Viscount.' Ulysses endeavoured to look conspiratorial and inebriated at the same time. 'Who would frisk a real, live lord?'

Hiram was exhilarated. He knew the identity of the courier. However, he shook his head and looked mournful.

'Believe me, Ulysses, he has no chance. They even searched the Pope for pot.'

'But, what you don't understand, Hiram, is that what comes in is harmless.'

And Ulysses proceeded to explain how the miraculous nectar was produced from an apparently innocent heather which could pass any inspection without causing the slightest suspicion.

Not long after he had obtained this information, Hiram suddenly remembered that he had a pressing engagement and hastily rose to go.

'Do you have to leave?' Ulysses asked sadly. 'I was going to tell you about an old acquaintance of mine called Herbie. You remind me of him.'

Hiram fled. He was so overjoyed by the information he had culled, he paid the bill for the drinks. Ulysses quietly finished his drink and went to phone Lucinda and let her and Brian know that Hiram had taken the bait.

'That's good,' Lucinda told him. 'I'm fairly certain that Hiram's hoods are on to Brian and me. Wherever we go, we appear to have company.'

'I made sure of that,' her uncle told her, 'by meeting you both while his boys were following me around. It's nice to know that we are dealing with such reliable people.'

But if Ulysses was in a contented frame of mind, Hiram was positively ecstatic when he surfaced that evening at Semiramide's apartment.

'What's got into you?' demanded the siren.

'I had a few drinks with Ulysses,' Hiram crooned.

'So that's a reason for celebration?'

Hiram kissed her: she recoiled.

'You are polluted! You stink like a bootlegger's wake.'

'Yeah, I have had a few drinks,' Hiram admitted. 'You see, when I was with Ulysses, I stuck to tomato juice and I had to wash the taste out of my mouth.'

'And Ulysses, he drank tomato juice as well? Remind me to sell my shares in any booze company.'

'Ulysses! No way! I kept filling him with Scotch until he didn't know what day it was. And, boy, did he talk!'

'So now you know everything about this drug of his?' Semiramide asked eagerly.

'Not yet. But I have enough information for us to set a pretty trap for him. I'll teach that peasant not to try playing games with me.'

'Be careful,' Semiramide warned him. 'You don't want to underestimate Ulysses: he's as cunning as they come.'

'I took him in the past and I'll take him again,' boasted Hiram.

'What have you found out?'

'First of all, guess who is bringing in the dope.'

Semiramide considered and shrugged her shoulders, 'Search me,' she invited.

'None other than your old boy friend, the Viscount,' guffawed Hiram.

'Gerald?' Semiramide was incredulous. 'I don't believe it. That guy was so dim he couldn't find his way to the little boys' room without a guide. Ulysses would never trust him with a million dollar consignment.'

'I had it from his own Scotch untaped lips. What is more, when the stuff comes in, it is harmless.' Hiram repeated what he had learned about the strange heather.

Semiramide was thoughtful. 'Are you sure that Ulysses wasn't fooling? Heather – that's some sort of a plant that ends up in honey, isn't it?'

'Seems that Ulysses has discovered a special strain. And the Viscount is flying a load of it in for us.'

'And you are going to snatch it at the airport without having to shell out the million, right?' enthused Semiramide.

'Wrong,' smiled Hiram. 'I want the source of the heather. What's the good of one shipment? Most of that I shall have to distribute among the boys as samples. Who would buy a totally new product without some proof of what it does? No, my sweet, we play along with Ulysses: we even pay him if it is necessary. We gain his confidence and arrange for a really big shipment. Just to make sure that everything is going nice and smoothly, you go along with Ulysses and find out where he gets this heather.'

'Me? What makes you think that he would take me?' Semiramide asked.

'He's very fond of you, isn't he?'

'You must be joking!'

'But if I were to pass some of this dope to you and you were to feed it to Ulysses, don't you think that he would become very affectionate and quite attached to you?' Hiram proposed.

'I see what you mean,' Semiramide was amused. 'I

could get one hell of a kick out of playing with a doting Ulysses. Boy, will he suffer!'

'I thought that you would get into the spirit of the thing,' Hiram grinned. 'Once you know how we can get supplies from Ulysses, we get rid of him.'

'And the big shipment?'

'When he brings that one in, I'll have it seized by the narcotics cops. I have a couple of them on the pay-roll and for a piece of the action, they'd rape their grandmothers.'

'But, Hiram,' Semiramide objected, 'you said that when the stuff arrives it is harmless heather.'

'That's right, but nobody will know.' Hiram exulted in the revelation of his master-stroke. 'Before the heather can be analyzed, it will be stolen.'

'Stolen – from the cops. Who is going to snatch hot merchandise from under the noses of the narcotics boys?'

'I am, of course, or rather some of my friends,' corrected Hiram. 'That's when the boys in the narcotics squad earn their bread.'

'And we don't have to pay off Ulysses because he won't be able to deliver,' Semiramide cried, as she grasped the implications of the plot.

'You've got it,' assented Hiram. 'Of course, when the evidence disappears, the cops won't be able to hold Ulysses. But by then, we shall have his heather for nothing and be in a position to arrange our own collection and distribution. He'll be finished and we'll have every dealer in the States – maybe in the world – having to come to us for supplies. God, just think how rich we shall be!'

They gazed at each other, dazzled by their, as yet, imagined wealth.

Semiramide was the first to come out of her trance.

'Say, what are you going to do about Hamblewood?' she asked.

'Who cares?' Hiram was scornful of such trifles. 'Maybe we'll keep it for weekends if Gerald doesn't come up with the money. You know, this coup has put me in the mood.'

And he began purposefully to remove his clothes.

'O.K.,' sighed Semiramide, 'but will you do one thing for me?'

'Anything you say, baby,' Hiram was expansive.

'Take off your fucking socks!'

CHAPTER 13

Nobody told Viscount Hamblewood that he was under observation and he would not have believed them if they had. The glorified sex fun-fair aspect of the great house was supervised by Sarah and, more discreetly, by Miles. Gerald retreated into the life he understood, a world of flower beds and orchards, of pig sties and stables. The two representatives of the New York underworld who had moved into the country inn which was the nearest thing to a hotel that the village of Hamblewood possessed were not exactly unobtrusive. Their button-down shirts, soft felt hats and dark glasses, which they apparently never removed, suggested that they patronized the same tailor and outfitter as the late Al Capone. The villagers stared at them, dogs barked when they passed and babies whimpered in their cots. But Viscount Hamblewood was not the most observant of men and his mind was on more important matters; marrows not mobsters dominated his waking hours. Even if the Mafia had staged their own version of the Olympic Games in the area, he would have remained blissfully unaware of anything unusual taking place.

The two visitors were perplexed for they, in turn, could not perceive any break in the Viscount's routine. Everywhere he pottered, they pried. When he went into the village or one of the nearby market towns, they were close on his heels, their enormous hired Cadillac blending into the surroundings as successfully as the Empire State Building would tone into the landscape of Oxford or Stratford-upon-Avon. Yet, although they never relaxed their vigilance, the Viscount made no move which could be construed as collecting the suspect heather and he made no attempt to leave the neighbourhood, far less flit across the Atlantic.

Hiram received the reports on Gerald's inactivity with growing impatience. The deadline for Ulysses to deliver was fast approaching and that worthy was still conspicuously displaying his presence in New York. Semiramide made things worse by tactlessly suggesting that Ulysses had somehow fooled him. Hiram silently vowed that she would be dumped, along with Ulysses, as soon as she had carried out her allotted task and exhausted her usefulness.

Back in their hotel, Brian and Lucinda also waited nervously. They carefully avoided meeting Ulysses but stayed in touch by phone.

It was a fine evening. Lucinda glanced at her watch and called Ulysses.

'He should be landing in half an hour. I was thinking of going out to the airport to meet him.'

'That would be a very bad idea.'

'But why? Ever since your night out with Hiram, neither Brian nor I have been under observation.'

'You mean that you haven't noticed anybody watching you.'

'Yes,' Lucinda admitted, 'but I'm fairly sure that we are not being followed.'

'I think that you are right. I hope so since you will have to pick up the parcel. But it is just possible that Hiram is keeping an eye on the airport, particularly on flights coming in from London, so why take a chance? He's a big boy and can find his own way from JFK to the city without having you there to hold his hand.'

'But if there is any trouble?'

'Calm down. There won't be any trouble. And if there were,' added her uncle, 'what could you do about it?'

Reluctantly, Lucinda had to agree that Ulysses was right and she settled down to wait while the minutes ticked away. An hour passed: she was pacing up and down like a caged animal.

'You might as well sit down and have a drink,' Brian informed her. 'I just phoned TWA and the flight is about an hour late.'

Lucinda swore but resigned herself to her vigil. Brian found some restful music on the radio but it did not have the desired soothing effect and Lucinda turned it off.

The phone shrilled and she darted across to answer it. It was Ulysses.

'Oh, it's you,' she groaned in disappointment.

'I take it from your voice that you haven't heard anything yet.'

'No. Brian says the flight has been delayed.'

'He probably told you that to calm your nerves,' commented Ulysses. 'Don't worry, he will probably call you soon. When he does, let me know. I'm not in the hotel – too many people keeping an eye and possibly an ear on me. I'm at a nice, friendly bar, so ring me at this number.'

He gave her the number and hung up.

She had hardly replaced the receiver when the phone rang again. Lucinda took the call and the tension lifted from her face as she heard his voice.

'Paul! You're back safely! Are you all right? Have you got the heather? Did you have any trouble?'

'Honey! Give me a chance, one thing at a time,' Paul laughed. 'Yes, I am O.K. Yes, I have the heather. No, there were no problems, everything went according to plan.'

'Nobody spotted you?'

'No, relax! There were a couple of hoods, watching the place, but the only person they were interested in, for some reason, was your father, Lucinda. As arranged, your brother met me and handed me the plants. I declared them when I landed. Some custom guys looked them over and wanted to know why I was bothering to bring ordinary heather into the country.'

'What did you tell them?'

'I said that I had a Scottish girl friend who was homesick, so I had brought her some genuine Highland heather from the moors right by where she lived.'

'And they were happy?'

'They practically wept in their handkerchiefs. One of them had an Irish wife and I was afraid that he was going to ask me to give him a plant for her. Luckily, she was away on a trip, so he didn't bother.'

'My Uncle Ulysses insists that you do not bring them here, just in case anybody is watching the hotel. I have to get them from you in the next two or three days. Can you think of a good place to meet?'

'Sure,' Paul replied promptly. 'I had expected something like that ever since Ulysses asked me to go to England to collect the goods. The hostel is too exposed: everybody sees everything.'

'What about The Black Cockatoo?'

'I don't think so. That Semiramide woman goes there regularly. I have a better idea. Do you know the Juillard Room?'

'No.'

'There's no reason why you should since it has only recently been opened. It's a small recital hall, holds a couple of hundred people and it is the venue for hopeful, young pianists and others to make their classical debuts, before they can aspire to the big halls, Carnegie or Avery Fisher, you know. Well, this Thursday, I am performing there.'

'You mean the day after tomorrow?'

'That's right. It is my first public concert.'

'Really, Paul? That's wonderful! Can I come?'

'You'd better. That is where I intend to hand over our botanical treasure. It's a lot less obvious a rendezvous than some smoke filled dive in the Village and I can guarantee that the programme will not attract Semiramide. What do you say?'

'It sounds great.'

Paul gave her directions how to get to the hall and details of the recital.

'Can I come over and see you before?' Lucinda asked.

'I would love that, but I guess that I need every minute for practice before the recital. It will be my first public performance as a serious soloist: there will be some important critics and it can make or break my career. And this jaunt to England has made me fall behind schedule. Will you forgive me?'

'Of course, it was selfish and thoughtless of me after the time you have sacrificed for something which was never your problem.'

'Oh, no, Lucinda. I was pleased to do it. And, after the recital, that's different. There's nothing that I would like more than to have some time with you then.'

Brian listened to Lucinda's half of the conversation but said nothing. As soon as Paul had finished, Lucinda called

Ulysses and gave him the glad tidings. He approved of the suggested meeting place and warned her not to try and see Paul until the recital.

'Of course not,' Lucinda answered. 'Do you think that I would do anything as foolish as that?'

Ulysses phoned Hiram and arranged to meet him on Thursday evening, at the same time as Lucinda would be at Paul's recital. This, he reckoned, would draw the full attention of Hiram and his friends onto himself.

They met in a quiet art gallery on Madison Avenue.

'Seems strange, seeing you in a cultural setting,' Ulysses remarked to Hiram who was studying an abstract canvas with a look of blank bewilderment.

'Never mind the crap,' replied Hiram. 'Give me the stuff and let's get the hell out of here. These things give me the creeps.'

'I haven't brought anything with me,' was Ulysses bland reply. 'Does that trifle of a million dollars mean anything to you or has it slipped your mind?'

'Oh, yeah,' Hiram smiled weakly, 'but you don't expect me to pay up before I have the goods, do you?'

'And I thought that you trusted me.' Ulysses shook his head in mock dismay. 'I tell you what we do. Tomorrow, I bring you a couple of plants and I show you how to prepare the nectar. You can see for yourself that the heather is O.K. Then, while I am there, you order your bank to pay mine. As soon as I hear that the money is in my account, I hand over the rest of the consignment.'

Hiram considered for a minute then assented.

'Seems fair enough,' he said. 'After all, what we are both looking for is the series of big shipments that come afterwards. But when do you expect your brother-in-law to arrive?'

'Gerald? What's he got to do with it?' Ulysses asked innocently.

'You said that he would be bringing the plants in.'

'You must have misunderstood me, Hiram. I remember our chat. I said that it was an advantage to have an aristocratic relation. That's true but I would never trust him with something important. After all, Hiram, you have met him, would you entrust him with anything as valuable as this?'

Annoyance, frustration and resentment rendered Hiram speechless and he emitted a faint gurgle which Ulysses cheerfully accepted as a sign of agreement.

'Thought that you'd see things my way,' Ulysses said. 'Now, while I enjoy your scintillating conversation, I am too busy to stand about, discussing Viscount Hamblewood's intelligence, or rather his lack of it. Where do you want the plants – the Deare Center?'

Hiram nodded.

'Fine. I'll be there with them tomorrow morning at ten.'

'Can't we make it later?' Hiram protested. 'I don't function that well before midday.'

'Ten is the latest. I want our meeting to take place while the banks are still open in Switzerland so that you can put through that phone call,' Ulysses retorted. 'You'll have to go to bed nice and early tonight. And, this evening, you have to do some shopping.'

Hiram stared at him, puzzled.

'It's simple enough, man. We are going to produce a drop of nectar from the plants so you will have to visit an ironmonger and buy a few things. Nothing complicated, the sort of things that even my brother-in-law could buy without getting confused.'

Ulysses gave his list of required utensils and then

dismissed Hiram before he had recovered his wits sufficiently to ask any questions or raise objections.

While this encounter was taking place, Lucinda was in the Juillard Room. Although the hall was not full (it never was for an unknown artist's first recital) there were enough people in the audience for her not to feel conspicuous. She looked carefully at the audience but saw nobody who aroused her suspicions. There was the usual buzz of talk and rustling of programmes. The long, ebony Steinway grand piano stood open under bright lights, dominating the small, intimate hall. The house lights were dimmed and Paul walked onto the platform.

It was the first time that Lucinda had seen him formally dressed and he looked more handsome than ever in his sober, dark suit. He took his place at the keyboard after acknowledging the faint patter of applause which greeted his appearance and waited until there was complete silence. Without any fuss, he launched into a group of Bach 48 Preludes and Fugues. This was a different Paul from the youth who provided entertainment at The Black Cockatoo or from the very private person who had breathed his love song to Lucinda through the tormented notes of Chopin, in the seclusion of his room. He played the Bach with a quiet assurance, bringing out the strands of counterpoint with clarity and a sense of purpose. When he stopped, there was a new warmth to the applause.

He played some recent American music – Copeland, Virgil Thompson and Elliott Carter. But the central work was the huge Beethoven 'Hammerklavier' Sonata, one of the crowning works for the piano, demanding immense emotional concentration and technical virtuosity as well as sheer powers of endurance. The audience sat, enrapt, as the young pianist wrestled with the colossal work, wringing from it anguished outbursts of drama, pathos, grief and ultimately triumph. It was a moving performance, earnest and unostentatious, sincere and sensitive and with a mastery of the structure of the work which would have done credit to an artist of more mature years.

At the beginning of the recital, Lucinda had felt a pang of nervousness for Paul but hardly had he commenced playing when that disappeared and she found herself totally engulfed in the waves of magnificent sound. Nevertheless, she felt relief when the last chords of the Beethoven died away. The audience was unreservedly enthusiastic: Paul took several bows and then had a short break before winding up the programme with some lighter short pieces which showed off his fluency and brilliance. Once more there was great applause, clapping, even some shouting and whistling. To a man, the audience rose to their feet, stamping and cheering.

Inevitably, Paul had to play an encore. The audience grew hushed as he settled once more at the piano. Very deliberately, his eyes sought out Lucinda and then he started to play the same Chopin Nocturne, the work which, no matter how many other people might be present, belonged to just the two of them. It was his thoughts and his feelings, reaching out to her, and her alone. She could not wait until she could be with him again on their own.

When, at last, Paul was permitted to leave the platform, Lucinda hurried back to the artists' diminutive changing room. There was already quite a crowd beginning to congregate but he dashed across to her and handed her a canvas bag.

'I'm so glad that you could make it,' he said in a loud voice. 'I particularly wanted to see you: I have some lovely plants for your aunt's garden. I brought them along, hoping that you would be able to get here.'

He thrust the bag into her hand and whispered, 'I can't stop. I have to be civil to my professors and these guys from the press. Can you be at my place in a couple of hours?'

Lucinda nodded, thanked him for the horticultural exhibits which she knew that her aunt would prize greatly and beat a rapid retreat as Paul was swallowed up in the fast growing huddle of journalists and academics, impatient to offer their congratulations or to put questions to the star of the evening.

Lucinda got back to her hotel where she found Brian and Ulysses waiting for her. Her uncle seized the bag and the precious plants, gave her an absent minded and avuncular peck on the cheek and rushed off.

'Do you want to go out for a meal?' Brian asked.

'No, thanks. I have a date.'

'Paul again?'

'Let's not go over that once more, Brian, said Lucinda coldly, 'Paul has crossed the Atlantic twice, smuggled in dope and given up days he needed for practice to help us. Is it surprising that I want to spend an hour or two with the guy?'

Brian turned away angrily.

'I'll see you in the morning.' He dismissed her with a gesture of unconcern.

It was nearly midnight when Lucinda picked up Paul from his hostel. He had changed into more casual clothes but his face still showed signs of the great strain to which he had been subjected. He kissed her lovingly, almost gratefully.

'I have missed you,' he informed her. 'And, am I glad that tonight's show is over!'

Lucinda had brought the car and they drove to a quiet cafe which stayed open late. After a leisurely dinner, they went back to the hotel where Lucinda had taken the precaution of moving out of Brian's suite into a room of her own. Only when the door had closed behind them, did Lucinda have the impression that Paul was really back with her. She went to his arms and stood there for a long minute, breathing in his closeness, letting the days of their separation fall away. She cared nothing for the machinations of Ulysses, the villainy of Hiram and Semiramide, the stupidity of her father or the possessiveness of Brian. All that mattered was her desire for Paul and his for her and the fact that, at last, they were together again and alone.

'By the way,' she said, almost as an afterthought, 'you played beautifully tonight.'

'Yes,' Paul reflected. 'It felt pretty good.'

'And were you thinking of me while you played?' Lucinda's tone was half serious, half mocking.

'Only during the Chopin,' Paul told her. 'When you play something like the Beethoven, the composer takes over and nobody else matters. His emotions and his struggles become your own: somehow your fingers have to give expression to his ideas and his personality.'

There was an earnestness about Paul's response which convinced Lucinda that he was a completely dedicated artist. Even if he were madly in love with her, his music would always come first. She was proud of his talent and his accomplishment, yet she could not help feeling a twinge of jealousy of his art.

'Now you really are the great virtuoso,' she teased, 'you will be off on world tours and beautiful women will be swooning at your feet all over Europe and America.'

'Not yet I'm afraid,' Paul laughed. 'I have only just made a start on my career. Maybe, if I get good notices, I'll be invited to do a few more recitals and only then will come the chance to play a concerto with one of the great orchestras in a big hall. It will be years before I have a name that will pull anything like a public – that is if everything goes well. So, until then, I guess I'll have to be satisfied with a fan club of one.'

He kissed her again.

'I had better make the most of you then, before there is any serious competition,' Lucinda said, as she ruffled his hair affectionately.

She turned down the lights and found some quiet, dreamy music on the radio.

'Does that bug you after the serious music you've been playing?'

Paul shook his head with a smile.

'No, that's fine. It's simply an agreeable background, like pretty wallpaper. I find it helps me relax.'

'That's good. I want you to take things easy. Shall I fix you a drink?'

'I don't want anything. Stop fussing over me and come and sit down.'

Paul led her to the sofa, but Lucinda pulled him back gently.

'The bed is more comfortable,' she murmured, 'and more relaxing.'

Paul took a shower and then, swaddled in a thick woolly towel, he joined Lucinda in the bed. She nestled her naked body against him, absorbing his warmth, letting her hands play over the contours of his body. The mere fact of being with him felt good, bringing her a deep sense of contentment. She had known quite a lot of men during her life but with none of the others did she enjoy the same sensation of being completely at her ease as she experienced at that moment with Paul.

He stroked her shoulders and fondled her breasts, his flesh firm against her softness. They had no need for words and, lulled by the soothing music, they melted together. Lovingly, Lucinda took his swelling erection in her hand and massaged him until he could bear it no longer. He eased out of her grasp and slowly moved down her, kissing and caressing every inch of her rosy skin until he had buried his head in the fragrant, downy silk of her pubic hairs. She felt his tongue, venturing into her, arousing her and fluttering over her wildly aching clitoris.

'Take me now,' she whispered. 'I want you so much.'

He arose and as he kissed her mouth, she tasted her own sweet yet sharp aroma. She felt him, probing deeper and deeper into her vagina, moist and velvety, drawing him in until they were perfectly fused together. She closed her legs around his muscular haunches, clinging to him and squeezing him tight. He swayed back, lifting her effortlessly so that she was looking down at his face, the brightness of his eyes and the tiny droplets of sweat over his lip. They shifted until they were comfortable in the new position and she rode him, proudly, pressing down firmly as he thrust upwards.

'Oh, my darling,' Paul moaned.

Then, as she forced herself onto the great, rigid column, he came suddenly and mightily. The excitement of his gushing inside her brought her immediately to her own climax, a wild and wonderful palpitation which seemed to go on for ever. Gradually, the two of them subsided and they lay, side by side, peaceful and, for the moment, satisfied.

They made love twice more during the night. Each time was different but each time it was just right. Paul had an uncanny ability to detect every change in her mood and to respond exactly as she needed.

They were tired but they had no desire to sleep. They both sensed that the time would come when they would have to part and it might happen soon. The few hours or days which were left to them were too precious to be wasted. It was Paul who gave voice to their shared thoughts.

'I suppose that you will be going back to England before long.'

'Some time. It depends on how Ulysses manages in dealing with those two crooks. But that need not be the end for us, darling.'

Paul said nothing.

'We will be able to meet again.' Lucinda felt mounting alarm. 'Paul, you can come to England or I'll fly here. This is too good to lose: it must go on. Say it will be like that,' she begged.

'That's what lovers always say,' Paul answered softly, 'but they drift apart. You have your own life, Lucinda. I could not visualize you becoming the wife of a black concert pianist, wandering from city to city, staying all the season in one hotel after another and playing second fiddle to a grand piano.'

She did not know how to answer him. What he said was true but this was not the moment to face up to reality. So she kissed him tenderly.

'Don't talk like that. We're both tired. Let's get some sleep, my sweet.'

CHAPTER 14

The Deare Center at ten the following morning presented a far more peaceful appearance than at the termination of Ulysses' previous visit. He was accompanied by Brian despite Ulysses' insistence that he had no need of an escort. Brian had argued that it was possible that Hiram would bring some of his toughs into the meeting with a view to grabbing the heather. Although Ulysses had pointed out that such a course would be too stupid even for a moron such as Hiram to pursue, Brian refused to stay behind and eventually Ulysses had been obliged, albeit with bad grace, to permit him to come along. Brian was conscious that the true reason that he was eager to get out of the hotel so early was that he had no wish to confront Lucinda. He suspected that she had passed the night with Paul and the prospect of possibly having to gaze at the two of them over the breakfast coffee pot did not appeal to him.

As they tramped up the path, the birds carolled a welcome. By contrast, Hiram's greeting was decidedly down-beat. He had not got round to shaving and his bristling stubble was as unprepossessing as his bleary eyes. The bright light of the morning was even less kind to Semiramide. She had presumably spent the night at the Center since she was still wearing a frilly nightdress over which she had slipped a rather grubby dressing gown. Her scowl was calculated to chill the bravest heart but Ulysses was unabashed and he complimented her on her matinal freshness. She ignored his hypocritical salutation.

'What's this jerk doing here?' she enquired, jabbing her thumb at Brian. 'I thought that he was selling bedsheets or bedpans.'

'I see that you have brought your grandson,' Ulysses replied cordially.

He gave a friendly nod towards a strapping monster of a man who completed the party.

'Oh, that's Boris,' Hiram explained. 'I asked him to

look in in case we needed him. Have you brought the plants?'

By way of answer, Brian took a couple of clumps of heather from the bag he had been carrying. Hiram examined them dubiously. He turned his attention to Ulysses.

'You wouldn't be trying to pull something on me, would you, pal? I mean, this vegetable seems harmless.'

'If you brought the equipment I asked for, we shall produce some nectar for you. Then you can judge how innocuous the heather is,' Ulysses replied.

'O.K. If you say so. I'll send Boris home.' Hiram's tone was conciliatory.

'No, let him stick around,' Ulysses told him. 'He might come in useful later.'

The plants looked like any other heather but Ulysses pointed out that there were tiny sacs beneath the spiky leaves. These, he explained, contained a milky fluid which was the basis of the revolutionary aphrodisiac. Under his supervision, they stripped the leaves off the plants and threw away the useless stems. The leaves were then put into a deep aluminium pan and crushed. He then added some water.

'Do you have some alcohol?' he asked Hiram.

'Sure, like you said. I brought some brandy. Will Three Star do?'

'Anything. It is only to speed up the reaction. When you want to produce nectar in quantity, you will need a bigger mixing pan and let the stuff stand for at least a day to ferment. We are going to make a small amount in a hurry. Right?'

Hiram nodded, watching carefully every move Ulysses made in case he slipped some secret ingredient unseen into the mixture.

When the mash had stood for half an hour, Ulysses carried the pan into a kitchen. Here, he placed the brew on an electric stove and heated it.

'After a while,' he said, 'this will come to the boil. You will see that it will give off some light brown fumes. The trick is to trap them in a funnel and let the distilled liquid run through the glass tubes you have provided and collect it in a flask. It's as simple as that. However, I suggest that you get yourself a small still – there must be some of your old acquaintances, Hiram, whose family connections stretch back to the bootlegging days and who are expert in producing mountain moonshine.'

There was a tense silence as everybody watched the gooey mess which was beginning to bubble in the pan. Only Ulysses seemed unconcerned. Hiram hovered over the rudimentary equipment, intent on spotting any sleight of hand. As Ulysses had predicted, vapour was swirling up into the funnel and the first droplets of the distilled nectar misted the glass tubing.

It took some twenty minutes for the last of the fumes to be driven off from the pan and the liquid gathered into the flask. Ulysses threw away the mash of leaves and water and led the way back into the small office, carrying with him the flask which contained the precious fluid. He pointed to the phone.

'Make the call now,' he ordered. 'Time to pay.'

'Now wait a minute,' Hiram protested. 'I haven't seen whether this stuff works.'

'You will,' Ulysses reassured him. 'If you are not satisfied, you can cancel your instruction to the bank. But, you won't get the rest of the shipment until the million is safely in my account, just like we agreed.'

Boris cast an enquiring look at his boss in case this was the occasion for him to move into action, but Hiram, although complaining petulantly, did as Ulysses instructed.

'Now, I hope you are satisfied,' he said as he hung up. 'I still need to be convinced.'

'Say, Hiram,' Ulysses' tone was extraordinarily friendly, 'I'm parched. How about all of us having a cup of coffee?'

Hiram stared. 'Coffee? Why?'

'Hiram, we need coffee,' Ulysses told him firmly. 'Let Semiramide go and bring four cups.'

'Let Boris go,' snapped Semiramide.

Boris half rose, but Ulysses stopped him. He turned to Hiram and said emphatically,

'Tell Semiramide to go. The coffee will taste all the sweeter, coming from her fair hand.'

There was something in his expression which persuaded Hiram.

'Go and get it,' he ordered Semiramide. 'You know where to find the cups and where they hide the sugar in this dump. Go!'

Semiramide was indignant: she swore fiercely, but she went.

'So, what was all that about?' Hiram asked as the door closed behind her.

'Do you want me to try this stuff out on you or her?' Ulysses demanded testily, pointing to the amber liquid in the flask.

Enlightenment spread across Hiram's features. Boris, on the other hand, registered nothing. From his coat pocket, Ulysses produced a glass dropper, the sort of thing which is used to dispense nose drops. He inserted it into the flask and drew off a little of the nectar. When Semiramide returned, bearing a tray on which stood four steaming cups of coffee, the dropper lay concealed in the palm of Ulysses' hand.

'Boris could have got it,' she said sulkily, 'the damned coffee comes from a machine.'

'Before you sit down,' Ulysses ventured, 'haven't you got some cookies?'

'Goddammit!' she exploded, 'I'm not some kind of servant.'

'That's right,' Hiram was placatory. He got to his feet, crossed the room and kissed her. While Hiram's body screened him from Semiramide's view, Ulysses quickly slipped some of the nectar from the dropper into the cup of coffee which was in front of her.

'So, what goes with your heather juice?' Semiramide wanted to know.

'I'm waiting for the flask to cool. When we've had our coffee, it should be ready,' Ulysses explained.

Semiramide snorted.

'Drink up,' Hiram commanded, 'and let's get the hell out of here! As far as I am concerned, this is the middle of the night: I could do with another hour or two in the sack.'

Boris obediently drained his coffee in one enormous gulp. The other men imbibed in a more decorous manner, watching Semiramide all the time. She sipped her cup of the brew that cheers. She wrinkled her nose appreciatively,

'Not bad,' she commented. 'That's about the best instant coffee I've tasted.'

'Time to make a move,' Ulysses breathed to Hiram, as Semiramide finished the beverage.

Taking his cue, Hiram walked to the door.

'You boys come with me. We'll go into one of the wards and find a volunteer to try the stuff on.'

'That's right, you go this time,' Semiramide growled. 'I've done enough running around.'

'Quite right,' assented Hiram. 'You take it easy; we'll

be back in a minute. Boris, you stay here and keep the lady company.'

He scuttled through the door, followed closely by Brian and Ulysses. Once they were outside, Hiram locked the door with the key which he had abstracted, unnoticed by Semiramide.

'Nice thinking,' Ulysses complimented him.

They did not have long to wait before some strange noises began to emerge from the room. There was the thud of overturned furniture and a confused banging, howling, shouting and breaking of china. Amid the din, they were able to make out the voice of Semiramide.

'Take off your pants and give me that huge cock!' she yelled.

The obscure grunts of Boris might have signified compliance or objection and they got no clue to his behaviour from the succession of further sound effects of splintering wood.

'Have you never remarked that our Frankie has a somewhat vulgar strain in her character?' Ulysses asked Hiram.

'Fuck me!' screamed the lady in question on the other side of the locked door.

'She sounds as if she's sure got the itch,' Hiram observed.

The noises off rose to a mighty crescendo. They heard the tattoo of fists pummelling the door.

'Let me out of here!' shouted Boris. There was stark horror in his voice. 'This dame's gone crazy. It ain't safe here. Send for the cops! Do anything, only do something. Please, lady, let go of that. I promised my old lady that I wouldn't fool around no more. Please, she'll murder me – if you don't do the job first.'

These last remarks were clearly directed to his roommate. They were followed by the unmistakable sound of ripping cloth.

'Christ! Now how am I supposed to be able to walk out of here with my pants torn in two?' Boris's plea was of no avail. There was a smothering sound, as if some monster had overcome its prey. Then, silence, apart from the slithering of a heavy body against the floor and a series of groans, moans and the noise of heavy breathing.

Ulysses shook his head sadly.

'Poor fellow, he never stood a chance.'

Hiram mopped the perspiration from his brow.

'O.K. The stuff is genuine.' He shuddered at the thought of the mayhem which was being committed on the other side of the thin wooden partition. 'Maybe we ought to move: I'm not sure how long that door will hold. So, Ulysses, how much can you ship in and when?'

'That I shall tell you when my bank has confirmed that the money is in my account. Come along, Brian, I don't think that there is anything further that requires our attention and I would hate to be around when Boris eventually gets out of there. You'll be hearing from me, Hiram. Oh, and thank Semiramide for the coffee, won't you.'

CHAPTER 15

Saturday was always a busy day at Hamblewood except for those occasions when the house and grounds were deluged by the rain which Divine Providence decrees should fall in England on public holidays and those days appointed for tennis at Wimbledon, cricket at Lords and the major events in the flat racing season.

This Saturday, the sun had shone and sightseers had flocked through the gates in droves. When the last of them had been seen out and the house was shut for the night, Miles was heartily sick of his fellow men. He did not participate in guiding visitors around, but wherever he turned there would be a band of camera toting Japanese or sweating Americans, guidebooks in hand, peering at him and his environment. The sex side-shows made matters worse. His temper had not been improved by the behaviour of his father. Only a few days remained before Gerald was due to pay Hiram off or submit to Hamblewood becoming an annex of the ghastly Deare Center. Also, in ten days time, Melanie would be returning to the bosom of her family, fresh from her triumphal progress through North America, and her reaction on discovering that the ancestral dwelling was in hock to an unsavoury character from the New York underworld and was currently being used as a money making bordello was a prospect which made Miles flinch and turn pale. Logically, his father, being the cause of the catastrophic turn of events, should have been yet more panic stricken. But this was not the case. The Viscount still sported his shabby tweed jacket and soft cap when Miles judged that the traditional sackcloth and ashes would have been more appropriate. And his sole topic of conversation when Miles had encountered him that afternoon had been whether they could afford to have some of the stables and pig sties repainted. When Miles had broached the subject of their impending doom, his father had dismissed the matter as if it were of no consequence.

'You don't need to worry about that,' he said airily. 'Your Uncle Ulysses has taken it in hand. Capital fellow! He'll come up with something.'

So, now, as the last Honda roared away up the drive

and the staff started to collect the scattered bits of paper, plastic containers and empty bottles with which the departed horde had decorated Hamblewood, Miles was sitting miserably in the library. Sarah's pregnancy had taken a peevish turn and her husband was contemplating the attractions of deserting hearth and home and seeking some light distraction in a Trappist monastery.

Far off, in the bowels of the house, there was the faint ringing of a telephone. Shortly afterwards, the impressive bulk of the butler, Thistlethwaite, loomed in the doorway.

'I beg your pardon, Mr Miles, but there is a gentleman who wishes to speak with you.'

Miles groaned. 'Now what! If it is some idiot who wants to discuss providing us with pig sties fit for heroes to live in, let him babble to my father. Say I've emigrated to a convict colony.'

'I do not think that is the purpose of the caller,' Thistlethwaite replied. 'The gentleman informed me that he was speaking from New York.'

'That will undoubtedly be the grisly Watergate phoning to remind me that doomsday draws near,' Miles reflected bitterly. 'Has he been hanging on for long?'

'I fear so, sir.'

'Good. I hope that the call costs him a small fortune and he contracts bubonic plague. Can you catch plague from a telephone, Thistlethwaite?'

'I have never heard of a case, sir.'

'Pity. I suppose I shall have to talk to him. All right, Thistlethwaite, switch the call in here. My cup runneth over!'

'Very good, sir.'

The butler made a stately withdrawal and Miles waited abject, until the phone in the library sounded.

Miles took the phone. 'Yes,' he said.

'I am putting the gentleman through,' announced Thistlethwaite in measured tones. 'He does appear to be extremely displeased at having been obliged to wait, sir.'

There was a click.

'Is that you, Miles?' Three thousand miles did nothing to diminish the fury and impatience in Ulysses' voice. 'Does everybody who wants to talk to you have to wait for hours while your comic butler waddles over the house, or is that a privilege reserved for close relatives who are having to pay for a call from the other side of the globe?'

'I thought that it was Hiram,' Miles explained in relief. 'I was nerving myself to receive sentence. I've heard nothing from you for days or weeks and I presumed that you had foundered, taking my high spirited sister and her devoted friend with you.'

'Stop drivelling, boy!' Ulysses commanded. 'You'll soon be as bad as your father. It's cost me a fortune to talk to your butler and now you start reading sermons over the phone. I gather from your mournful tone that you have not organized some sensational way of dealing with Hiram. You haven't won a national lottery, stolen the crown jewels, held the Chief Rabbi for ransom or found some other legitimate way of raising Hiram's blood money?'

'No. Lucinda's sex jamboree has given a lot of people enormous pleasure but it has failed to fill the coffers.'

'How much do you have towards the million?'

'Only four hundred thousand dollars, I'm afraid, and we don't have any time left.'

'You can stop worrying.' There was a new refreshing jauntiness about Ulysses. 'It happens that I have pulled off a business venture. Lucinda will give you all the distressing details when she sees you. Tell me the name of your bank and I shall send you the six hundred thousand dollars you still need. Then it will be up to you to make sure that you get back from Hiram that contract which your brainless poop of a father signed. Your legal training should be adequate for that. But make sure that Gerald does not get his hands on the money and keep him well away from buxom blondes, at least until his wife is back to restrain his unnatural sexual appetite.'

'That's marvellous news. I truly had given up hope,' Miles said. He gave Ulysses the details of his bank account and then added, 'It seems a strange coincidence that you should have laid your hands on the exact amount of money which we required.'

'I never said that. I made a little more, but I shall keep the balance to defray expenses. I did warn you that this would be an expensive phone call.'

And with that, Ulysses hung up.

The following day, Miles got to work to redeem Hamblewood. Ulysses was as good as his word, so Miles was able to offer Hiram the full million dollars which had seemed a few hours ago to be an unattainable goal. Getting back the contract turned out to be unexpectedly easy. Hiram appeared to have lost interest in Hamblewood and was ready to fall in with conditions which Miles laid down. It was ironic that the two participants in the great swindle were both preoccupied with other matters of greater moment. Hiram's eyes were firmly fixed on the immense wealth which would be his as soon as he had the nectar trade properly under control while his dupe, the too-trusting Viscount, was absorbed with the practical problems of redesigning and decorating the accommodation which was afforded by the Hamblewood estate for its resident pigs and horses.

The coolness between Brian and Lucinda persisted and Monday breakfast was a subdued affair. Ulysses was aware of the strained atmosphere; he made few efforts at conversation and as soon as he had gulped down a couple of cups of coffee, he disappeared from the scene. As he left, he called over his shoulder,

'Make sure that you are both here for lunch at one. I have a little business to attend to which concerns you.'

'How are things going with Hiram?' Brian asked listlessly.

'Be here on time and you'll find out,' was the terse rejoinder.

Brian wandered out and did some desultory shopping. Lucinda hung around the hotel, glancing moodily at magazines and wasting time. There was no point in trying to contact Paul since she knew that he would be tied up all the morning with classes. When Brian returned and a short time later, after they were rejoined by her uncle, there was no sign of the gloom lightening.

Ulysses glared at them. 'Here,' he said, throwing an envelope onto the table, 'I have brought you a present.'

Lucinda opened the envelope. Inside were two first class tickets for the flight the following evening to London.

'What's the idea?' Brian demanded.

'The idea is that the two of you get back home,' snapped Ulysses. 'I have sent sufficient money to Miles to pay off Hiram.'

'So the game is over,' Brian said.

'It's over as far as the two of you are concerned. For me, it has hardly begun,' Ulysses told them.

Lucinda had been examining the tickets.

'I don't think that I am ready to go yet,' she said deliberately.

'You will do as you are told,' replied Ulysses indignantly. 'Our dealings with Hiram have up to now been fun. From now on, things might get rough and I don't want the two of you around as either targets or possible hostages.'

'If you expect trouble, we could help,' Brian offered.

'The only help you can give me is to vanish without making any fuss.'

Lucinda seemed about to raise a further objection, but Ulysses cut her short.

'When I offered to get you out of your spot of trouble, it was a condition that you did as I told you.' His tone was that of a field marshal putting a surly private soldier in his place. 'I have delivered. Now, the pair of you, shake the dust of New York from your heels before you spoil my play with Hiram. Can't you get it through your heads,' he cried in exasperation, 'you'll just be in the way – a couple of bloody liabilities!'

Brian looked hurt and Lucinda not fully convinced. Her uncle concentrated his attack on her.

'Do you realize that your mother will be home within a few days? When she gets there, she is going to discover that her stately home has been converted into a second class imitation of Coney Island. Don't interrupt,' he shouted as Lucinda opened her mouth. 'And that fun fair was your idea, wasn't it, Lucinda. So, you had better be there to help your long suffering brother in his hour of need. It will require the two of you to prevent my sister from dismantling your father into his constituent atoms and molecules. So, get moving!'

Lucinda regarded Ulysses sullenly. Then, without a word, she picked up one of the tickets, nodded in mute assent and went up to her room.

Ulysses wheeled on Brian.

'I don't know what's got into you two, but I can guess. I haven't got the time for this romantic crap. How you make out with Lucinda is your affair. But, you make sure that she is on that plane tomorrow night even if you have to hit her over the head with a gin bottle. In a short time, Hiram will not be in the mood for jokes. Is that clear?'

'All right, you've made your point,' Brian answered. 'Lucinda is headstrong, but she's not stupid. She won't be around to queer your pitch.'

Late that afternoon, when he returned to his hostel, Paul found a message waiting for him to call Lucinda urgently.

'Say, what's the matter?' he asked. 'I was going to ring you when I got back anyway.'

'I must see you,' Lucinda told him.

'Sure, honey. How about dinner tonight? Tell me, what is wrong.'

Lucinda ignored his question.

'Pick me up at the lobby of the hotel at eight,' she ordered. 'You will be ready?'

'I'll be there.'

For the rest of the day, Brian kept out of Lucinda's way. He could tell that she was upset and he judged that anything that he might say or do would only make things worse. When Lucinda announced that she was taking the car for the evening, neither of the men raised any objection. She took a shower and chose her clothes with care. When Paul arrived, a quarter of an hour early, she had been downstairs waiting for twenty minutes. Brian, sitting in the lounge, saw the tall, young pianist stride into the lobby and kiss Lucinda with an ardour which indicated that this was no casual meeting. They left the hotel immediately: Brian remained in his chair, his face a study of misery and bad temper.

Outside, Paul asked Lucinda where she wanted to go for dinner.

'I don't care,' she replied irritably. She threw him the

keys to the car. 'Here, you drive. Take me anywhere you like: only let me get away from here.'

They drove in silence. Paul chose an intimate little restaurant which had recently opened, looking onto the Park. It was still relatively unknown and he was certain that they could get a quiet corner where Lucinda would be able to tell him what was on her mind.

She waited until they were nearly through the meal. Then, abruptly she told him that in less than twenty-four hours, she would have left the United States.

He took her news calmly.

'I have been expecting this,' he said. 'It had to come sooner or later. Once I had seen that palace in England which is your home, I knew that there was no way that you would stay on here.'

'You don't understand.' Lucinda was annoyed that he appeared to consider her too much of the moneyed aristocrat to be prepared to accept New York. 'Ulysses insists that we leave.'

'We? You mean you and Brian?'

'Yes. But this does not have to be the end for us, does it, Paul?' Her eyes were pleading with him and she gripped his hand hard. 'After all, there is no reason why you should not come to England, is there?'

'And throw up the rest of my classes at the Juillard School? You realize that would mean ending my career as a musician before it had even started? Is that what you want, Lucinda?'

'No, of course not.' Tears were pricking her eyes but she fought them back. 'But I don't want to lose you.'

'Come now, my darling. What do you really want? Be honest, would you want me around all the time, a husband, or at any rate a full time stud? Would you want to keep yourself exclusively for me?'

She wanted him more than ever at that moment but she could not deceive him any more than she could fool herself. Sadly, she shook her head.

'No, you know me too well. But, what we have is too good to let it finish like that.'

'What we have is too good for us to pretend to each other,' he replied. 'I don't live in your world, Lucinda, and you don't live in mine. We have been brought together by a marvellous fluke and we have taken our chance. It's been great and I don't want to spoil it by playing some role in the future which is not my true self and neither do you.'

'I guess I ask too much from life,' Lucinda sighed. She would have liked to argue with him, win him over, but, in her heart, she knew that he was right. Paul would not be happy in the traditional setting of Hamblewood and she was not cut out for the part of life companion to a concert virtuoso.

'At least, you could come and pay a visit some time when you have completed your studies,' she whispered. 'Say you will, Paul, it will give me something to look forward to when I am back in Hamblewood.'

'Sure, why not.'

He knew that he never would and so did she. But the promise which would not be kept made their parting more bearable.

Paul took her back to the hotel. They went to bed and made love tenderly, almost wistfully. Lucinda shut her eyes and tried to fix in her memory every moment. She wanted to be able to remember always the feel of his hands over her body, the light which shone in his eyes when he looked at her, the subtle yet strong scent of his body. He was her ideal lover, at once strong yet tender, young yet mature, taking her but giving himself absolutely, holding back nothing. Her body shook in the rapturous throes of a mighty orgasm and the whole wide world beyond the strong arms of her man which encompassed her, ceased to exist.

Yet she knew, even at that instant of sheer ecstasy when they were so completely united and immersed in each other, that the moment was fleeting and they were destined to drift apart. For each of them was too strong a personality to be merely a subject of the other. If he were not so much an individual in his own right, she could not have loved him as she did, but this very ruggedness of his character and of her own would inexorably drive them into the fulfilment of their own potential and into living their own lives. He brought her supreme happiness in the wonder of their bodies, but her sorrow could not be dispelled and it haunted her slumber.

She was still more than half asleep when she felt the brush of his lips against hers and when she awoke, he had already gone. It was better that way: protracted farewells would have been too painful and would have been an anti-climax after a night during which everything had been said wordlessly, in the miracle of their love.

After breakfast, Ulysses was far less taciturn in making his adieus. He explained that for the rest of the day, he would be tied up with Hiram and Semiramide and so he would not be able to see them off.

'However,' he informed them sententiously, 'I anticipate that I shall be paying a flying visit to the United Kingdom within a very few days and I shall look in at Hamblewood and check that everything has gone according to plan.'

'It will be great to see you again,' Lucinda said and she kissed him. 'It seems strange that such a short time ago we considered you Public Enemy No. 1: I've got quite fond of you.'

'So you should. I am your uncle, you know. As for the past, perhaps I did not exhibit the more charming aspects of my sweeter self. Take care of yourselves and, whatever happens, do not miss that plane. The New World has no further need of you.'

'Wait,' Lucinda called, as he went to leave. 'We ought to pay you for the tickets.'

'Don't give it a thought,' Ulysses answered with a wave which dismissed the matter as of no consequence. 'You will find the bill for the hotel has been settled. That, and the fares, regard as a little present. I am feeling in a generous mood. Take advantage of it while it lasts.'

'This adventure must have cost your uncle a bomb,' said Brian, after Ulysses had departed.

'I'm not so sure,' Lucinda mused. 'He did not look like a man who has made a great sacrifice.'

It was not until they were on their way to the airport that Brian mentioned Paul. Lucinda had been a bit withdrawn throughout the day but, now that they were about to return to England, Brian had recovered from his bout of bad temper.

'Is Paul not coming to the airport?' he asked.

'I guess not.'

There was silence and then Lucinda continued,

'I did not want him to come. No tears at the barrier and that sort of thing.'

'He wasn't a bad chap,' Brian conceded, 'but, you know, he wasn't the man with whom you could settle down.'

'Settle down? What are you talking about?'

'You know what I mean. Go steady for more than a few weeks.'

'Brian, can't you get it into your head that I am not

what you would call the settling down type? I value my freedom and I shall never belong to any man.'

'That's the way you feel now.' Brian was sympathetic but there was a trace of condescension in his manner, as if he were older and wiser than her, which riled Lucinda. 'You were fond of the guy, but that will pass and, one day you will find that you are looking forward to settling down with the right man.'

'Meaning you, I suppose?' Lucinda answered icily.

'Wait and see,' was Brian's reply.

PART IV

'penurious Heaven
With a too sparing hand has given
A plant but seldom to be found,
And thrives but ill on British ground.'

(The Inquisitive Bridegroom)
WILLIAM SOMERVILLE

CHAPTER 16

When Ulysses had dismissed Brian and Lucinda, he had returned to his suite. He had several things to attend to before he would be ready also to quit New York and he put through a number of phone calls. The first of these was to Hiram to check on his progress in treating the heather. Hiram had encountered a few problems in setting up his mini-still. Ulysses attempted to sort them out and he promised Hiram that he would stay in the hotel in case further consultation was necessary.

A couple of hours passed without any call from Hiram and Ulysses assumed that the Watergate distillery was now satisfactorily on stream. He called Brian's room and was informed by the receptionist that he had checked out and that both he and Lucinda had actually left the hotel. Ulysses decided to celebrate by having a pot of tea sent up to his room.

A few minutes after he had ordered the festive brew, there was a gentle knock on the door. Ulysses opened it in order to let in the waiter, but it was Semiramide who was standing in the corridor. She had taken considerable pains over her appearance and was wearing a smartly cut two piece suit of soft dove grey which gave her an unexpected aura of quiet good taste. However, Ulysses' reaction to this apparition lacked cordiality.

'What do you want?' he demanded.

'Aren't you going to ask me in?' Semiramide countered.

'No,' said Ulysses.

She smiled sweetly at him and pushed her way past. She

chose the most comfortable armchair, settled down in it and proceeded to take a cigarette from her bag, light it and puff smoke idly at her inhospitable host.

'And how are you passing your time now that Hiram is playing with his chemistry set?' Semiramide asked.

'Before this unwelcome interruption,' Ulysses replied, 'I was enjoying my own company.'

'Dull,' commented Semiramide. 'You should be able to do better than that.'

Ulysses had no chance to vent his wrath on his visitor: the waiter arrived with the tea.

'Bring another cup,' Semiramide ordered.

As the waiter left, she beamed at the glowering Ulysses. 'That's hardly what I would have expected you to be drinking.'

'I'm rehearsing for England,' Ulysses snapped.

'Now, that is precisely what I want to discuss with you.' Beneath her amiability, there was an undertone of seriousness and Ulysses regarded her closely. 'You see, I think that it would be a good idea if we made the trip together.'

'Kind of you to offer to keep me company,' Ulysses responded gruffly, 'but I am quite capable of managing on my own.'

They were interrupted by the return of the waiter with another cup and saucer. Semiramide helped herself to tea and poured a cup for Ulysses.

'I suppose Hiram has sent you to shadow me,' Ulysses grumbled.

'You, Ulysses dear, are most decidedly on the wrong track. What do you want Hiram in on this nectar business for?' Semiramide had dropped the casual pose completely and she rapped out her staccato sales talk. 'You know that Hiram can't be trusted: at the first opportunity, he'll turn you over.'

'And you wouldn't?' asked Ulysses sarcastically.

'Why should I? Think. You are giving Hiram the chance to make millions. Why?'

'You know very well. He has to handle the distribution here in the States while I look after the supply side.'

'Sure,' retorted Semiramide with an air of impatience, 'you have to have somebody over here. But why Hiram, who will cut your throat the moment it suits him? I can look after the distribution for half what Hiram is screwing you for.'

'Yeah, I'm certain that you would. However, it happens that Hiram knows all the big pushers and you don't.'

'That doesn't matter. You know that this stuff is not like any old dope; it's unique. You know that when Hiram has processed the plants you gave him, he will distribute most of the nectar as free samples to the leading distributors. Once they have tried it and have seen its effects, they will buy from whoever has the stuff. Cut out Hiram and we don't have to go looking for the pushers; they'll come to us, begging for the new wonder dope and willing to pay whatever we ask. Believe me!'

'So I should ditch Hiram and team up with you?' Ulysses gave her a sour smile.

'That's right. Call it self defence: if you don't get Hiram, he'll get you.'

'But I thought that you and he were partners?' Ulysses said.

'Hell, no. I worked with him but he treats me like dirt. Here, let me show you my bruises.'

Semiramide raised her skirt and started to roll down her tights but Ulysses stopped her.

'Please, no. I've seen enough of your bountiful supply of flesh to last me a lifetime and I couldn't face another display on an empty stomach.'

'Does that mean you're inviting me to dinner?' Semiramide asked eagerly.

Ulysses ignored the suggestion. 'Tell me,' he demanded, 'if you are prepared to turn on Hiram like the treacherous bitch you are, why should I trust you, partner?'

'It's not the same with you,' Semiramide protested. 'Hiram has really ill treated me: he's weird, sadistic. Not like you, Ulysses. Sure, we've had our differences but you've always been fair with me and I swear that I'll never try to pull one of Hiram's tricks on you.'

Ulysses snorted in disbelief. 'Drink your tea, it's getting cold.'

He got to his feet and walked across the room. As soon as his back was turned, Semiramide whipped out of her bag a small bottle. She unscrewed the stopper and was on the point of pouring the contents into Ulysses' cup when he wheeled around and seized her wrist.

'Not this time, sweetheart! You keep your love philtre to yourself.'

Grabbing her by the scruff of her neck, Ulysses yanked her to her feet and bundled her out of the room. Apart from a vain attempt to bite his hand, giving voice to a string of oaths and obscenities and violently kicking and thumping the door from the outside, Semiramide departed with dignity.

However, if Ulysses believed that this was to be the end of his liaison with Semiramide, he was mistaken. Wherever he went, he had the impression that he had grown an extra shadow. But it must be said, that Ulysses, for his part, made no strenuous effort to evade his pursuer or throw her off the scent.

One more call to Hiram verified that he was happily ensconced among his bubbling retorts and flasks.

'Get moving on a regular supply,' Hiram ordered.

'I'm on my way,' Ulysses assured him.

So, a few days after Brian and Lucinda had made their exit from the States, Ulysses took his place in the British Airways night flight, bound for London. He fastened his seat belt and settled down for hours of boredom. Sidling into the next seat, Semiramide gave a half apologetic smile.

'Here we are again,' she simpered.

They ignored the in-flight movie and moodily demolished the dinner which was placed before them. Ulysses pulled a rug over his legs and closed his eyes. He found it impossible to sleep and he summoned a stewardess and ordered a brandy.

'And one for me, too,' Semiramide called to the stewardess.

Ulysses had left his seat and gone to the toilet when the drinks arrived. Semiramide looked around swiftly and took her opportunity. By the time that Ulysses had resumed his seat, she had replaced the tiny bottle in her coat pocket.

Ulysses sniffed his drink suspiciously and looked hard at Semiramide. She shrugged her shoulders and swapped glasses with him. Ulysses considered for a moment and then changed the glasses back.

'I don't know whether you are bluffing,' he told her, 'or is it a double bluff?'

'We would get on much better if you had a more trusting nature,' she said in a tone of wounded innocence.

Shortly after he had drunk his brandy, Ulysses was aware that he had made a mistake. The throbbing insistence in his crotch was unbearable.

'I imagine that you are ready to reconsider my proposition,' she gloated.

Ulysses pulled his rug up to his waist and, under its cover, he set about massaging his affected region.

'Let me do that for you,' Semiramide offered. Her hand burrowed under the rug and took possession of his swollen penis. 'My, aren't you a big boy,' she commented.

The lights had been dimmed in the cabin and most of the passengers were endeavouring to snatch some sleep. Ulysses let his seat down until he was reclining in as near a horizontal position as possible. He made a tentative grab at Semiramide's thigh, but she brushed his hand away.

'This time, I call the shots,' she told him. 'I want you nice and submissive.'

All the time she was talking, Semiramide continued to rub Ulysses' mountainous erection. Now, she gave it a firm tweak, as if to assert her authority. He winced but was unable to pull away from her fingers which were kneading and moulding his flesh and insidiously controlling his will.

'So, let's be a team on this heather gig.' Her voice was soft and persuasive. 'I swear I only slipped you a tiny drop of the juice, just enough to make sure that you would listen to what I want to say.' She tightened her grip a shade and accelerated her coaxing motion, smiling with satisfaction as Ulysses responded, twisting and turning in his seat like a tortured soul.

At that moment, the stewardess returned. She smiled sweetly at Ulysses.

'Is there anything else I can get for you, sir?' she enquired.

Semiramide glared at her, balefully.

'Piss off!' she hissed.

Ulysses eyed her lustfully: his voice was hoarse.

'Come and join us,' he entreated.

The plane happened to make a slight jolt and Semiramide accidentally jerked aside for a second the rug which had up to then concealed Ulysses' predicament. The stewardess gazed in mingled horror, amazement and fascination at her passenger's swollen member which seemed to beckon and to menace her. Ulysses made a clumsy grab at her but she eluded his grasp and beat a hasty retreat down the aisle away from his lecherous hands.

Semiramide hauled him back into the seat.

'Listen, buster,' she threatened, 'I intend to keep you fully occupied and when I've finished with you, you won't be capable of even looking at another broad for a month.'

With a moan, Ulysses subsided and resigned himself to the inevitable. For a minute or two, Semiramide was silent and let her hands do all the talking. She considered that she had things once more under full control and was on the point of resuming her business proposition when a bald, rosy faced man wearing a loud check shirt approached. He was about to stroll past when he became aware of Ulysses who was squirming beneath his rug like a flea bitten serpent.

'Pardon me, sir,' he exclaimed, 'but I happen to be a doctor and you appear to be in some sort of trouble. Can I be of service to you?'

Without waiting for a reply, he pulled aside the rug to examine his patient's afflicted anatomy. His timing could not have been more unfortunate.

For, at that very moment, Semiramide's ministrations came to a climax and so did Ulysses. The well meaning practitioner was rewarded for his concern with a geyser of hot sperm which gushed into his face and cascaded down his picturesque shirt.

Semiramide regarded his florid features with amusement.

'My,' she observed, 'you look just like some new kind of Christmas pudding with a very special cream sauce topping.'

The outraged man of medicine staggered away in the direction of the toilets, mopping himself furiously with a large handkerchief. Such was his confusion that he even forgot to demand a consultation fee.

Although Semiramide protested that Ulysses had imbibed only a niggardly dose of nectar, this torrent brought him no relief. Scarcely had his cock descended than it was once more splendidly erect like a signal at a particularly busy railway junction. Semiramide got back to work.

'Feel like a serious chat?' she asked.

Ulysses' reply was a strangled groan.

'I meant what I said about Hiram intending to double-cross you,' she continued. 'But this could be our big chance. Don't you want to settle down, Ulysses? Me, I've had enough bumming around with an asshole like Hiram. I'm not getting any younger and as soon as he has you and your heather in the bag, he'll drop me for some dumb teenage chick. Don't you see, Ulysses, we need each other!'

By way of answer, Ulysses emitted a grunt of disbelief: at that moment, he was incapable of much in the way of eloquent conversation.

'It's true,' Semiramide pressed her point, emphasizing her logic with her fingers. 'Think for a moment. Since you were involved with that affair on Xanthos and all those kids were lured away from their homes, your name has been poison in the States. I could keep the contacts going with the customers where you would be about as welcome as a fully paid up member of the Society for the Spreading of Leprosy. You need somebody: all your time will be spent in getting the supply side organized. And with the money we make, we can buy a little place somewhere quiet and rural like Beverly Hills.'

'And you think that Hiram would let us live in peace in our country cottage after we pull something like that on him?' Ulysses managed to gasp.

'I guess we may need to take a few precautions like hiring a dozen or so body-guards to live in.'

'And what happens when we go out?'

'So we invest in a bullet proof limousine.'

Imperceptibly, Semiramide had been working him harder and quicker and now, Ulysses clutched wildly at her and she felt his penis quiver and then thrust spasmodically as he ejaculated.

'I think you had better have those pants cleaned and pressed when you get to London,' Semiramide remarked philosophically as she removed her hand and wiped it dry.

It was a few minutes before Ulysses felt sufficiently recovered to resume their dialogue.

'So your idea of a simple life in the country is a house with a battalion of gorillas, all armed to the teeth and an armoured car to go and collect provisions.'

'We could get rid of Hiram permanently, if you preferred,' Semiramide assured him. 'It would be cheaper. It's up to you, honey: whichever way you want to play it.'

'Never mind the details,' Ulysses replied thoughtfully. 'I've decided to accept your suggestion. From now on, we're partners. Right?'

'Right!' enthused Semiramide.

'I can rely on you, as long as there is a profit in the arrangement for yourself,' Ulysses said. 'And, you are right. The operation is more than I can handle on my own.'

'Sure, and if anything were to happen to you – like you fell ill or met with an accident – '

'Yes, I appreciate the point,' Ulysses interrupted. 'So you come along with me and we get the heather together.'

Semiramide was in a contented frame of mind when they straggled out of London Airport into the steady downpour of rain with which visitors to Heathrow are customarily greeted. Ulysses, his raincoat buttoned over his ravaged trousers, had thawed to such an extent that he was holding her hand as they dashed into the taxi.

The next few days were hectic but everywhere that Ulysses went, Semiramide remained in close attendance. Ulysses made no attempt to conceal his preparations from her and he showed a friendly, good humoured side to his nature which had never been revealed to her previously.

She was in high spirits when she put a call through to Hiram. He was understandably terser since, in New York it was five in the morning.

'That's O.K.,' she replied when Hiram protested at being aroused at such an unearthly hour. 'You can catch up on your beauty sleep later. I haven't time to hang around until you are out of bed and it's important that I talk to you today, so listen.'

Hiram spluttered, but she shouted him down.

'Like you said, I've stuck to Ulysses and he hasn't been able to make a move without my seeing. The sucker has fallen for that story about him and me working together and I know everything.'

'Great!' Hiram revived on the news. 'So where does he get that heather from?'

'I'm coming to that. I can tell you that he will be bringing in a hell of a lot of plants. We've been buying a couple of huge, wooden crates and he has had them lined with moss, to keep the heather fresh. Flying them in would look too suspicious: who would spend that amount of money on freight for some lousy common weeds? We are booked, along with our crates, on the next voyage of the QE2.'

'The what?' asked the still sleepy Hiram.

'The Queen Elizabeth, you know, the ship. Do pay attention, Hiram!'

'Yeah, yeah, and where are these wonder plants now?'

'We are going to collect them tomorrow evening. Ulysses has hired a station wagon and we have spades and lanterns – '

'Lanterns?'

'Sure. He says we have to lift them in the dark.'

Hiram was by now quite awake. 'Wait a minute. If you are sticking so close to Ulysses, where is he now? How come you are able to make this call without him knowing?'

'Because today, I've let him go off on his own. Don't panic, Hiram, I know what I'm doing. He is paying a visit to Hamblewood and we know that, whatever else goes on there, my beloved Gerald doesn't run a dope plantation. And Ulysses has left the crates behind: there's no way he could sneak all those plants back in without my seeing. No, this is his family call. Tomorrow, we get the plants together.'

'So when will you be back here?'

'In exactly ten days time. Can I rely on you to have a reception committee standing by?'

'You just make sure that he delivers and that you know where he gets the plants. Leave everything else to me,' Hiram chuckled.

During the next couple of days, Hiram put in a lot of calls. He had got rid of all the nectar which he had distilled from the first shipment and now he summoned a meeting of the bosses of the chains of dope distributors throughout the country to whom he had given his samples. Without exception, they reported that they had been impressed by this revolutionary new product and were keen to buy.

Not too far away from New York, on one of the major turnpikes, stands the 007 Motel. Hiram had used it before for discreet meetings and he rather liked the way one could hire suites, all of which were named after some famous espionage network. He had entertained in KGB, CIA and M15 formerly. This time, he decided on Mossad in preference to BOSS and the Deuxieme Bureau, since it was larger. So they came, the sinister men who ran the underworld and Hiram exulted. This was the Big Time and they were all dancing attendance on him. Orders were taken and terms of payment and delivery hammered out. The amounts involved were astronomical and by the conclusion of the negotiations, Hiram was exhausted but he felt ten feet tall. The others had left, but he stayed on. His work was not yet finished.

The two men who arrived long after the others had departed had insisted that they did not register in their own names.

'Fine,' Hiram had said, 'Who shall I expect? Mr Smith and Mr Jones.'

'Don't be flippant,' was the reply.

They had indignantly rejected Dr Jekyll and Mr Hyde and it was as Mr Benson and Mr Hedges that they introduced themselves to the clerk on the reception desk.

'Where there's smoke, there's fire,' had been his comment.

'Do you think he suspects something?' Mr Benson asked Mr Hedges.

At a prearranged signal, they were joined by Hiram.

'This had better be good,' Mr Hedges warned him. 'We're taking a hell of a risk meeting you.'

'Relax. This place is secure.' Hiram exuded easy confidence. 'I take it that you boys are still in a position to watch over some drugs being brought into the country?'

'If you want something slipped in, we can handle it,' Mr Benson replied, 'but it will cost you quite a packet.'

'You misunderstand me,' smiled Hiram. 'I want the Narcotics Squad to seize a shipment. I have all the details of when and how it is coming.'

Mr Benson stared at Mr Hedges, then shrugged his shoulders.

'I suppose you want to get some guy into a spot of trouble. Well, that can be done, but it also is a service which does not come cheap. Depends on what sort of stuff he is smuggling. What do we look for, heroin, cocaine, you tell us.'

'Heather.'

'What?'

'Heather, like I said. Harmless heather.'

'If you've got us here on some sort of a joke,' Mr Hedges began menacingly but Hiram interrupted,

'And I am prepared to pay as if it were heroin.'

'You say this heather is harmless?'

'That's right.'

'Then what's going to happen to us when the lab boys analyze it?' demanded Mr Benson. 'They'll think we are screwy, seizing it.'

'They'll never analyze it,' Hiram said. 'After you've taken the crates, they will be stolen.'

'How?' asked Mr Hedges.

'That's where you earn what I am having to pay you. Arrange the snatch anyway you like, just as long as I have those two crates with their contents intact within twenty-four hours of your getting your hands on them.'

Mr Benson thought that there was something fishy about the scheme and did not want to have anything to do with it. Mr Hedges agreed. Hiram mentioned casually that it was a pity that they were passing up the chance to get very rich, since there would be more crates afterwards which would need shepherding through customs. On more mature consideration, both Mr Benson and Mr Hedges allowed themselves to be adjusted to take account of the unusual circumstances.

It was not until the early hours of the morning that they had finally settled all the terms and conditions. Hiram was not ready to call it a day before he was certain of the arrangements such as where the crates would be housed after seizure and the details of the robbery.

When everything had been agreed, his visitors ushered him out of their suite. Back in his own bedroom, Hiram retired for the night and was soon sound asleep with a seraphic smile on his face.

CHAPTER 17

On the day that Ulysses made his visit to Hamblewood, he found the house plunged into gloom. He was disappointed. He had anticipated that the redemption of the ancestral home would have resulted in wild euphoria, a brass band playing on the village green while merry yokels cavorted in strange folk dances and other manifestations of rural delight.

Nothing of that sort greeted him. His arrival was unannounced so he was not concerned at there being nobody at the station to meet him. It was when he actually entered the mansion that the chilling atmosphere became apparent. He was admitted by a sombre Thistlethwaite, but then the butler had always given Ulysses the impression of a funeral parlour attendant who had not been paid his rightful wages. He caught a fleeting glance of his brother-in-law who, instead of frisking merrily like a lamb, was about as festive as a slaughtered sheep. The sense of some solemn occasion was heightened by the Viscount having discarded his beloved old tweeds and being formally attired in dark suit, grey tie, white shirt and the sort of stiff collar which went out of fashion shortly after the demise of Queen Victoria.

'What's happened?' Ulysses demanded. 'Has one of your favourite pigs died?'

'Worse,' croaked the mournful noble. 'Melanie's home.'

'Do I take it from your shocked demeanour that the domestic arrangements did not meet with the whole-hearted approval of my sister?' asked Ulysses facetiously.

'There are not many things in this world of which she does approve,' complained Gerald. 'She read somewhere of this sort of sex fun-fair which we have been running at Hamblewood,' he explained in hushed tones.

'I can imagine that she was unsympathetic, especially as you could not tell her why you had been obliged to go in for that sort of fund raising exercise,' said Ulysses pointedly.

Gerald shuddered. 'Miles and Lucinda are trying to get her to see reason. They've been closeted with her for half an hour: they must be having a frightful time in there.'

'So why aren't you in the torture chamber with them? As the head of the family, you ought to be the first for the thumb-screws.'

'It's not that I am afraid,' Gerald's expression belied his words: he was terrified. 'I started to give her the account which we had rehearsed before her arrival, but she stated that she wasn't in the mood to listen to the drooling of an idiot.'

'Unkind, but I get her point,' Ulysses opined.

'So she collared the children and told me to wait outside.'

'Maybe that was for the best. You don't have the physique for a martyr,' said Ulysses by way of comfort. 'However, I don't have much time to spare, so I think I shall exercise my prerogative of the prodigal brother returned, and barge in. I may be able to help.'

'Why don't you wait until after lunch?' suggested Gerald. 'Melanie is always fiercer on an empty stomach.'

Ulysses explained that as he could only spare a short time at Hamblewood before getting back to London for urgent business, he would risk incurring the wrath of his famished sister and he ambled along to the Music Room where Gerald informed him the family conference was in progress.

He found Melanie sitting in judgement on her erring offspring. Her annoyance at being interrupted before sentence had been pronounced and carried out was tempered by her pleasure at seeing Ulysses again. She recalled that her brief meeting with him a few weeks ago had been an unexpectedly agreeable experience and Ulysses immediately switched on maximum charm.

'Forgive me for intruding,' he gushed, 'but I had no opportunity to warn you that I was coming and this is merely a flying visit. But, as I had to be in England for a couple of days, I had to find a few minutes to pass by and pay my respects.'

'That was good of you,' Melanie responded. 'However, you happen to have chosen rather an awkward moment. It seems that while I was out of the country, these children have permitted Gerald to commit some folly which I am now obliged to investigate.'

She glared at the accused rather as if she had caught them, red-handed in some act of high treason. Although

Miles was an able lawyer, he was showing signs of wilting under the strain of this cross-examination, while Lucinda had the air of a schoolgirl summoned before the Head Mistress for the first time in her career.

'You wouldn't be referring to this business enterprise of theirs on which I gave them a little friendly advice, would you?'

Melanie turned her attack onto her brother.

'You mean to say that you suggested converting Hamblewood into a house of ill repute?'

Ulysses laughed, 'No, I think that is something of an exaggeration. But don't forget, sister mine, that our family fortune was founded on the pioneering of mail order contraceptives. I guess that Lucinda has inherited our talent and will prove to be a worthy descendent of dear, old grandpa.'

Melanie was about to object, but Ulysses forestalled her.

'Just consider,' he warned, 'she might have taken after your husband.'

Melanie was rattled but she protested, 'Even so, this is no way to behave in Hamblewood itself.'

'That's right,' Ulysses assented. 'You have this enormous estate – all those fields and woods. Now that they have had a chance to start the business up and see how it works, it will be easy enough to reassemble the sexy side of Hamblewood somewhere in the grounds, a decent distance from the house. And, as for the Sex Supermarkets, they are all miles away. And, do bear in mind, Melanie, these things are profitable: they are really paying off.'

This was a new slant for Melanie. Ever since the day she got married, Hamblewood and her husband had absorbed money and had never provided a penny of revenue. The possibility that her aristocratic connection could also make a contribution to paying the tradesmen's bills was a revelation.

'Miles was saying something about having earned good money just when you came in,' she conceded but she wheeled on her son and jabbed an accusatory finger at him. 'So, what about tax? Have you considered that we'll have to meet a gigantic tax bill?'

'Not at all,' interposed Ulysses. 'I came here to propose to you that the operations should be acquired by a company of mine, Erotic Enterprises, which is established in a tax haven country. None of you need show – that is if you are willing to trust me with the financial management?'

The combination of good profits, negligible tax and the steadying influence of her sage brother, once a rascal but now, providentially, redeemed, was overwhelming and, after a proper show of reluctance, Melanie gave the arrangement her blessing. Gerald could not believe his eyes when they emerged from the Music Room, wreathed in smiles and without even a flesh wound in evidence.

Ulysses allowed himself to be persuaded to stay for lunch but shortly afterwards, took his leave.

Miles accompanied him to the station.

'You had better give me details of this company of yours, Erotic Enterprises,' he said.

'Sure,' his uncle agreed. 'I'll let you know as soon as it is formed.'

'You mean it does not exist?'

'Of course not, but it soon will. I had to invent something which would make the right impression on your mother, hadn't I?'

Miles had to hand it to his uncle for quick thinking and

the manner in which he had cut himself in on their thriving business merited his respect.

'Where can we contact you?' Miles asked, as Ulysses boarded the train.

'You don't. At least, not for a while. Don't forget, I still have an account to settle with Hiram T. Watergate and that will keep me out of circulation for a time. But, don't worry, my boy, you will be hearing from me quite soon.'

Miles had no notion just how soon and in how sensational a manner he was to get news of his unconventional uncle.

CHAPTER 18

It was a lot of work moving the (s)exhibits away from the main house to a hunting lodge, situated in the grounds at Hamblewood about three quarters of a mile away. However, it was a relief to Lucinda to have something to occupy her. Ever since her return from New York, she had been affected by that old restlessness which had afflicted her from time to time in the past when she felt that she had completed a stage in her life and was waiting for something to turn up, some new challenge.

She missed Paul. She wrote to him but there was no reply and when she tried phoning his hostel, she was told that he was away on a trip and had not left a forwarding address. The warden of the hostel who took the call thought that he had been invited to do a few recitals out of town.

Melanie had resumed control of the daily routine: it was as if she had never been away. Lucinda was despatched on a sequence of errands and social calls, but she found these depressing.

Brian was aware of her inner tension and did his best to divert her. But even their sex life became unexciting. Not that Lucinda was being distracted by some other affair: she was simply not suited for life without the spice of adventure, even danger.

The major part of the move to the hunting lodge had been completed and Lucinda was relaxing in her room. It was early evening, traditionally a dead time at Hamblewood after the departure of the last of the sightseers and afternoon callers and before pre-dinner cocktails. She was glancing listlessly at a book when Brian came in.

'I'm not disturbing you?' he enquired.

Lucinda shut the book and shook her head.

'I thought I'd go off tomorrow,' Brian informed her.

She merely stared at him.

'There's nothing much for me to do here,' he said defensively. 'I should look in on my folks: it's been years since I was last home.'

Lucinda's gloom deepened. With Brian gone and Miles and Sarah totally absorbed by Sarah's imminent delivery, the house would be more desolate than ever.

Brian seemed to be reading her thoughts.

'You don't have any time for me any more,' he said miserably, 'so I'll be better out of the way. You've changed, you know.'

He was so obviously wretched that she felt a wave of sympathy for him.

'You could stay on and help manage the sex supermarkets,' she suggested. It was a feeble effort and she knew it.

'You've got those so well organized now that you and Miles don't need me. It's not just a matter of finding something to do: I can get a job easily enough. It's us. Our relationship has sort of ground to a halt: do you know what I mean?'

'Come to me,' she murmured and she melted into his arms.

He held her tight. They stood there, reliving all the months they had spent together. He stroked her hair and kissed her eyes, her nose, her throat and then her lips: each embrace was a mute cry of farewell. She led him to her bed to surrender herself to the potent enchantment of his body for the last time. She wanted to feel his muscles, smell his own personal odour and imprint everything about him which singled him out as Brian, somebody special and unique, her man, on her memory, as if by holding on to the remembrance of him she could retain his physical presence.

As for Brian, he wanted her more than ever. He had no need of Ulysses' magic heather: the nectar of her lips drugged his senses. He covered her with his kisses, from her tiny, delicate feet to the shining glory of her golden hair. He could not bear to be parted from her and yet he knew that there was no way he could endure staying, now that she had drifted away from him. But he was resolved that nothing would spoil that last miraculous encounter.

And nothing did. When his lips closed around her taut nipple, she knew all the longing which was surging through him – how he desired the soft seduction which was promised by the creamy ripeness of her breasts, by those long legs, so sleek and slender, by the promise of the swell of her hips, full, rich and luscious. His hands moved across her body with the assurance and yet the reverence of some virtuoso whose touch was drawing from the depths of her being the most sublime music. But when he eased his proud phallus into her brimming, hot vagina, the melody of their love-making soared to the unimagined heights of bliss. For them, the flat, familiar world around them ceased to exist: they were all in all to each other and they floated in the clouds of their own ecstasy.

It had never been better, Lucinda never sweeter, Brian never more adoring. Their rhythm, as they swayed at first gently and then ever more fiercely was that of the dance which ever since the beginning of time had united men and women in the incandescent flame of passion. It was more than sex: it was a sacrament, each body consecrated by the other until they rocked in the infinite joy of their mutual orgasm. The wonder and the pleasure was all the stronger since, beneath the surface, there lurked always the sadness of their impending parting.

They never said a word all the time that they possessed each other: their emotions were too strong for the banalities of commonplace speech which would have jarred on the music made incarnate which their bodies were playing. And they knew, when it was all over, that even if their separation were to last for the rest of their lives, they had something which they would never lose, something precious which belonged to them and which nobody else could ever share. In each other's arms, drinking in the presence of the beloved partner, Brian could hear each heart beat of Lucinda; his breath was warm and moist on her skin. There had been an earnestness about their coming together which had made them feel that protracted foreplay would have been out of place but they luxuriated in the mellow marvel of the afterglow of their passion.

After a moment, or perhaps an eternity, Lucinda stirred and, with a sigh, broke the spell.

'We must make a move, Brian darling. Remember, it's Mummy's big night.'

A formal dinner party had been arranged as a homecoming for the Viscountess but she had refused to allow it to take place until the shameful trappings of the side-shows had been removed from the house and it had been returned to its pristine dignity. Even while Lucinda and Brian were re-enacting their drama of love and farewell, downstairs a livelier and far less exalted activity was in hand. Battalions of domestic servants were preparing the house, moving furniture, polishing china and glass, arranging flowers and bustling about in the disciplined and purposeful manner which comes from long familiarity with the protocol of the formal soiree.

'I don't think that I shall fit in with all the pomp and bullshit,' Brian said wryly.

'You'll be fine,' Lucinda reassured him. 'Melanie would never permit a guest in the house to be deprived of the caviare and champagne. Thistlethwaite is bringing evening clothes to your room. A house like Hamblewood keeps a supply of black ties, white shirts and all the rest of the paraphernalia for any stray passers by who stay for dinner. You had better go and get dressed up – we're all in uniform tonight.'

Brian left Lucinda's room to walk back to his own. On the way, he was stopped by a couple of unsmiling, brawny men in identical grey suits who frisked him for hidden weapons. Melanie, as befitted a prominent American expatriate, had invited the United States ambassador among the guests and his security officers had moved in.

Having changed into the dinner jacket and the rest of the accoutrements which had been provided by Thistlethwaite, Brian went downstairs. On his way, he was stopped and searched again by two different but in every way identical, Secret Service agents.

'Are you guys enrolled or simply cloned?' Brian demanded, after he had been pronounced clean.

'Beat it, buster!' came the diplomatic rejoinder.

A succession of limousines, mostly Rolls Royces but with a sprinkling of such lesser breeds as Cadillacs or Mercedes, decanted a selection of the cream of London society under the porte-cochère of the house, whence they were ushered into the cavernous ballroom where they were received by their stately hostess and her unhappy spouse. The Viscount infinitely preferred the company of pigs to peeresses but his place was at his wife's side, as she had commanded, shaking hands with people whose names he had forgotten and telling characters he had never set eyes on before how pleased he was to see them again.

As was usually the case when Melanie organized something, the dinner was a success, progressing smoothly from soup to soufflé without a hitch. Under normal circumstances, such formal evenings would be held in the family's town house, situated if not a stone's throw at least within mortar range of the American Embassy. That this was not the case this time was due to a request from the ambassador. He particularly wanted a discreet conversation with a number of influential people who would be among his fellow guests (his staff had seen to that) and it would be preferable to meet them as if by chance in a social gathering rather than in the embassy, where they would be under the scrutiny of the press and possibly other even more unwelcome observers. The boss of the posse of Secret Service agents responsible for his safety had insisted that the Farrer's London residence was far less secure than Hamblewood, standing in its own grounds which could easily be patrolled. So, Melanie, as befitted a loyal Daughter of the American Revolution, had changed the venue to their country seat.

Another factor on which the ambassador had shrewdly counted was, because of the remoteness of Hamblewood from London, most of the party would want to scuttle away as soon as it was decent to do so after the meal. Consequently, along with the bare minimum of his bodyguard, he was able to fade away into the library, where he was joined by the eminent men and one woman with whom he was anxious to talk, without the risk of being disturbed by stray intruders blundering in.

Some time later, when Melanie was graciously despatching her last duchess, the ambassador emerged from the library and went over to her.

'Lady Hamblewood, I am ashamed to say that having enjoyed your lavish hospitality and caused you a vast amount of trouble in diverting your reception to the country, I have another request to make.'

'What can I do for you, Mr Ambassador?'

'Our Secretary of State made an important announcement earlier today and I am most desirous to see how what he has said has been received in Britain by the media. A news bulletin is due in a moment: may I impose on you to watch television for literally five minutes?'

'Why, of course,' Melanie was still in the throes of escorting the duchess to the door. She turned to her daughter, who was standing nearby. 'Lucinda, please take His Excellency into the television room.'

Lucinda dutifully led the way and switched on the set. She waited while the ambassador listened to and watched the item which interested him. He rose to leave but Lucinda was gazing open mouthed in horror at the following report. There, on television, beamed across the Atlantic by satellite, in full colour was the image of her uncle Ulysses. The handcuffs around his wrists were clearly visible.

CHAPTER 19

Before Ulysses had permitted Miles to drive him to the station after his brief visit to Hamblewood, he had asked to see what remained of their stock of the heather. He regarded the dozen or so plants thoughtfully and Miles explained that they were about to bring some more in from the 'Lucifer' where they had a small store.

'Then, we'll have to go back to Xanthos to replenish,' he concluded.

'Don't do that. Not yet, anyway,' Ulysses said. 'What I would like you to do is as follows. Bring those plants up to London in the next few days and leave them in a case at Waterloo Station. Take the left luggage ticket to your club and put it in an envelope addressed to me. I'll pick it up later and collect the erica erotica which I need. Check up with your sister that she hasn't got any more stashed away. If she has keep them under wraps. Just don't merchandise any more of this lust liquor until I give you the all clear.'

Ulysses refused to tell Miles his plans but he extracted from him a solemn promise to obey his instructions on the moving of the heather.

Back in London, he found Semiramide waiting for him.

'How was Hamblewood?' she cooed. 'Did darling Gerald send me his love?'

Ulysses did not reply, but the way he looked at her spoke volumes. Swallowing down the acid rejoinder which sprang to his lips, he kissed her lightly on the cheek.

'Did you miss me, honey?' he enquired.

Semiramide eyed him suspiciously. She was not accustomed to such consideration from Ulysses.

'Have you been drinking?' she asked.

'Hell, no, Frankie. Forget this Semiramide jazz, to me you'll always be the same old Frankie.' There was a sentimental light in his eyes as he let his features relax into a smile which positively oozed cordiality.

'Say, what's got into you?'

'I've been thinking things over on the train back,' Ulysses informed her. His tone was serious and he commanded her attention. 'Sure, we agreed to be partners in shipping heather. That's business. But, the way I feel, our partnership goes deeper than that. We've known each other, on and off, for years and, at my age, a man gets round to considering settling down. And we old bachelors tend to get lonesome. Have I ever told you that you are a mighty handsome woman?'

'Say, Ulysses, what is this?' Semiramide breathed. 'Are you actually getting round to proposing to me?'

'Something along those lines,' he admitted. 'I know that when you gave me that dose of nectar we fucked like stoats but it was after the effect wore off, I slowly realized that I really appreciated you, not simply in bed as a sort of living mattress – '

'Mistress,' she corrected.

'Whatever you say, but I like having you around. So, what do you think?'

'Gee, this is so sudden.' Semiramide fluttered like a teenager facing the apparition of a love-lorn swain for the first time in her life. But then the practical side of her nature reasserted itself. 'It sounds a swell notion, Ulysses, but don't you think that we ought to concentrate on getting this traffic organized before we decide on anything definite?'

'O.K. But can I take it that you are not turning me down in a sweet, tactful way?'

'Oh, no, not at all. I really mean what I say. We'll be together and have a chance to see how things shape up.'

Ulysses kissed her again, this time with considerably more fervour. 'Fine,' he exclaimed. 'So, tonight we are going to celebrate. Put on your fanciest gown and I'll take you out for the greatest dinner in the world.'

'You mean it?'

'Of course. Tomorrow we start work in earnest, so let's make the most of this evening. Oh, and just one other thing, Frankie darling. When we get moving on collecting the heather, we shall be very busy, so please promise me, no more games with that little bottle of nectar which you have.'

'I prefer you as a natural lover, Ulysses,' she answered. 'However, I shall keep it in reserve in case you don't live up to your promise. It gives a girl a sense of security to have around a sure way of keeping her man nice and docile, should the need arise.'

Ulysses nodded understandingly. 'You had better go and get ready if we are going to hit the town. Shall I pour you a bath?'

'Do I have to bath?'

'I'm afraid that where I shall take you they would disapprove of unscrubbed bodies.'

Semiramide had always preferred indolence to hygiene, but she allowed herself to be overruled and was soon installed in a hot tub. She stretched her limbs languorously and regarded her copious charms. I'm still in pretty good shape, she mused. No wonder Ulysses has turned amorous. Still, he's not as young as he was. With some of the wonder nectar, I should be able to find myself a youthful stud and then Ulysses and Hiram and the other old farts like that stupid Viscount can all go and play with themselves. And she would be so rich! Life was pretty good.

When he heard her busily splashing in the bath, Ulysses smiled to himself; once a scrubber, always a scrubber. Stealthily, he removed from her bag the bottle of nectar and poured its contents into an ornamental flower pot where it nourished a startled house-plant. Just in case the need does arise, he chuckled. He refilled the phial with a mixture of cold tea and Bourbon which he found matched the colour of the nectar fairly well. By the time Semiramide emerged from the bath, pink, glowing and contented, the bottle was back in her bag and Ulysses was busy shaving.

He was as good as his word. The food at the Connaught was superb, the wine a treasure and the bill read like a ransom demand. Since Ulysses had a few pounds left, they went on to a night-club or two and Semiramide lightened his wallet further by some unwise speculation at a roulette wheel. She was looking forward to some good sex as a triumphant conclusion to the evening but she was so exhausted that she fell asleep as soon as her head hit the pillow. Ulysses sighed with relief and went to sleep.

The following morning, resurrection was an excruciating experience. But Ulysses was relentless and he nagged her until she was dressed and flinching in the morning sunlight.

'If anything were to happen to me,' he told her, 'you would have to arrange future deliveries of the heather yourself. So, it is important that you know all there is to know about the plant. I'm going to take you all over the country, starting with the great botanical gardens at Kew. You are going to see every kind of heather so that you will be able to distinguish between our heather and any other species which somebody might try and palm off on you. As I told you, honey, we're going to be busy.'

In the few days that were left before they had to

embark, Semiramide underwent a crash course in plant recognition. Worse, she had to endure the practical sessions, out at night on moors and heathlands, digging up plants – tall heathers, dwarf heathers, white heathers and purple heathers, bell flowered callunas and great gorse like plants that tore her hands and broke her finger-nails. All the specimens were carefully preserved by Ulysses so that they could be compared in daylight.

'Why do we have to dig up the entire English countryside at night?' Semiramide complained, staring at her blistered hands.

'We're lifting them from private estates where we have no right to be,' explained Ulysses patiently. His hands were in good shape since it was Semiramide who did the digging while he supervised.

'Which are our plants?' she wanted to know.

'I'll show you when we have finished.'

To Semiramide's relief, the day dawned when they were due to make their way to Southampton and board the QE2. She had completed packing her clothes and the souvenirs which she had collected to distribute to her friends.

'Let's get cracking on the plants,' she suggested.

Ulysses was looking at her thoughtfully.

'You know there will be a ceremonial dinner on the ship tonight. There always is, first night out. You really ought to be looking your best.'

'So what's wrong with me?' she bridled.

'Nothing, sweetheart, nothing at all. Only – '

'Only what?'

'Well, you know we shall be sitting with some very important people.'

Semiramide looked unimpressed.

'Aristocrats – maybe royalty.'

Semiramide still looked unimpressed.

'Very, very rich people.'

Semiramide was impressed.

'I thought that it would be nice if you had a good hair-do before we left.'

She fingered her hair. Now that Ulysses had mentioned it, her scalp itched and she was sure that her locks were lacklustre and lifeless. She was self conscious and ashamed.

'I guess there is a salon in the hotel,' she ventured.

Ulysses shook his head. 'Why not go to Maurice? He's the best. Everybody who is anybody goes to Maurice.'

'Say, how are you so knowledgeable, all of a sudden?' Semiramide's suspicions surged up.

'My sister is a viscountess,' Ulysses reminded her.

'Well, if this Maurice is so popular, I would have to book up days, maybe weeks, in advance.'

'That's why I booked an appointment for you as soon as we arrived.'

Semiramide was astonished. 'You mean you had the whole thing worked out?'

'It was necessary if you were to have your hair seen to by Maurice. Of course, if you would rather have it fixed by somebody in the hotel, I can cancel your appointment.'

'No, no, is he really that good?'

'You'll see. You will be the sensation of the ship: the captain won't be able to keep his eyes off you.'

Ulysses called a cab and bundled his companion off to her rendezvous with the coiffeur of the century. As soon as she had gone, he took a taxi himself. He called in at Miles' club and kept the cab waiting while he collected an envelope. Then he went to Waterloo Station where he picked up a case from the Left Luggage. He was back in the hotel long before Semiramide, radiant and elegant, returned.

She found Ulysses standing before the two wooden crates in which, protected by moss, she could make out heather plants.

'Good,' Ulysses greeted her. 'I wanted you to see before I nail the lids on these boxes.' He thrust in his hand and pulled out a plant.

'Aren't you going to say something about my hair?' Semiramide asked in a hurt tone.

'Sure, it's heavenly,' Ulysses replied curtly. 'But we don't have much time before we have to leave for Southampton. So, watch carefully.'

He held out the plant and pointed out to her the tiny sacs under the spiky leaves which contained the secretion that made this heather unlike any other in the world.

'That's why I wanted you to see what the other plants are like. None of them had those little blisters. Right?'

Her eyes glistened. The great secret was hers. Ulysses had shown her on a map where all the different heathers of the United Kingdom were to be found and she recollected every backache and lacerated hand. She peered into the other crate and pulled out a heather. She examined it carefully. There were those tell-tale sacs. Satisfied, she watched Ulysses hammer down the lids. It was about time that he undertook some of the physical labour, she considered.

On arrival at the docks, Semiramide installed herself within their stateroom and took charge of the arrival of the cases which they required during the voyage. Ulysses supervised the stowage of the luggage which was going into the hold, including the two crates. While he was so engaged, Semiramide picked up the phone.

'Can you put me through to a number in New York?' she demanded.

'Of course, madam,' replied the shipboard operator and a few seconds later, she was talking to Hiram. Hurriedly she told him the distinguishing marks on the crates and reassured him that she was in full possession of everything there was to know about the heathers. On hearing the news, Hiram overcame his morning lethargy and chortled that she could now relax and enjoy the sea voyage. He would be making all the necessary arrangements.

She had barely completed her call when Ulysses strolled in.

'Were you on the phone?' he enquired.

'No. That is to say yes,' Semiramide replied. 'It was one of the stewards who wanted to know if we would like a pot of tea in the room before we sail.'

There was a knock on the door. Ulysses opened it and a steward came in.

'We wondered whether you or your good lady would like a pot of tea?' he asked amiably. 'We won't be leaving port for another hour or so.'

'No,' snapped Semiramide.

'Yes,' Ulysses said.

The steward gazed at them. 'Just tea for one, then.'

'Make it for two,' Semiramide amended.

The steward fled.

'Strange that they should have phoned through a moment before a steward came to the room,' Ulysses observed.

Semiramide changed the subject hurriedly.

The voyage was uneventful. Semiramide was disappointed that they were not invited to join the captain's table on their first night out, especially as her hair was resplendent. Ulysses assured her that he had specifically requested that they should not be made conspicuous in any way since they were travelling incognito. Semiramide was not sure of the logic of that, but she let it pass.

On the last night, Ulysses seemed restive.

'What's worrying you?' Semiramide demanded.

'I was wondering,' Ulysses replied thoughtfully, 'exactly how we are going to get our precious cargo ashore without running into Hiram and his boy scouts. Then we'll have to hide away until you have had a chance to make contact with your buyers.'

Semiramide laughed. 'Don't you give it another thought. I made all the necessary arrangements before we left England. Sure, Hiram will be expecting us, but some of my friends will detain him on his way to the docks. Nothing too violent, you understand, but we'll have plenty of time to take ourselves off to where some other gentlemen will be waiting for us with their chequebooks at the ready.'

'My, you have been a busy, little girl, haven't you,' Ulysses said approvingly.

They went to bed early. Semiramide made no attempt to administer a dose of her love-syrup to her companion. She had no desire to have sex with him: once ashore, with that marvellous medicine, she would have her choice of boys and beaus. Ulysses was his normal well behaved self and did not require treatment to bring him to heel. Life was being kind to Semiramide.

Like young tourists, coming home for the first time from the wide world outside the States, they stood the following morning at the rail, watching the surrealist fairyland of Manhattan, emerging from the mist. All around them, there was the bustle and apparent confusion of passengers searching for their trunks, ship officers completing the formalities laid down by the Federal

Government and the even more detailed requirements of the New York Harbour Authority, once the huge ship had been nudged and jostled into her berth by the bevy of attendant tugs.

Once ashore, Ulysses looked around but, as Semiramide had promised, there was no sign of Hiram or any of his lieutenants. Semiramide stayed close beside him while he took charge of their luggage and, escorted by a trio of porters, entered the customs shed with their trunks and the two crates.

'Hey, you! Over here with all that stuff.'

Ulysses obeyed the order which had been shouted at him by one of two officials. Mr Benson smiled at Mr Hedges. Everything was going to schedule. When Ulysses looked around for Semiramide, she had disappeared with her own luggage.

'Open up!' Mr Hedges pointed at one of the crates.

'They are merely botanical specimens,' Ulysses protested, as the lid of the crate was wrenched off and Mr Hedges gazed at a clump of heather.

'We have reason to believe that these are narcotics,' Mr Benson stated. 'We are holding you, brother, and if these turn out to be what we think, you will have a long, flowing beard before Uncle Sam lets you out of the accommodation which he keeps for guys like you.'

'You can see that they are only heather plants,' Ulysses pleaded, but nobody was paying any attention to what he said.

Suddenly, he was surrounded by a multitude of reporters, television crews, customs officials, officers of the Narcotics Squad and a posse of the grimmest faced policemen Ulysses had ever encountered. While one of the cops handcuffed Ulysses, Mr Benson made a short statement to the assembled newshounds to the effect that they had intercepted a vast consignment of a mysterious and dangerous drug, that Ulysses was a notorious underworld figure and that the whole operation had been successfully accomplished thanks to information which had been laid by a zealous, virtuous and public spirited citizen. With that, cameras whirred and the shed was brilliantly illuminated by high powered lamps and flash-bulbs.

That was the scene which Lucinda witnessed on television at Hamblewood in the presence of the United States ambassador. Ulysses, having completed his involuntary TV appearance, was bundled into a police car and consigned to a cell to await his fate.

CHAPTER 20

The spectacle of Ulysses being led away, manacled, was the last that British viewers saw of what some excited reporters termed the drug sensation of the century. Consequently, Lucinda was spared the performance of Hiram on later news programmes. During these interviews, Hiram blushed modestly when he was congratulated on his courage and shrewdness in the face of great danger. For Hiram had explained that he had been infiltrated by agents of the Narcotics Squad into an international network of desperadoes whose leader was now safely behind bars. Hiram disclaimed the credit: it was no more than any decent, patriotic American would do, given the opportunity, he told viewers throughout the United States.

However, what she had seen was sufficient to galvanize Lucinda. She ran from the room, pushing past the ambassador who was beating a stately retreat and almost colliding with her mother.

'Whatever is the matter?' Melanie called out at her daughter.

But Lucinda did not wait to answer. She rushed, threading her way through the last of the hangers-on from the reception and the army of servants. She tracked down Brian and led him to a quiet corner where they could speak without being disturbed or overheard. In few words, she told him what had happened to Ulysses.

'You can't possibly go away at a crisis like this,' Lucinda's tone was both accusing and indignant.

'Calm down,' Brian answered. 'Of course I'll stay, if you think that I can be of any help. But I don't see what we can do for your uncle.'

'We'll have to fly back to America,' Lucinda said.

'There's nothing we can do tonight. Why don't we talk to Miles in the morning. As a lawyer, he ought to be able to tell us what can be done,' Brian suggested.

Miles was not very helpful. He warned Lucinda not to allow any more of the nectar to be distributed while the heat was on Ulysses and told her that there was absolutely no action they could take before formal charges were laid against their unhappy uncle.

'And don't come out with any of your crackpot schemes for some sort of romantic rescue – snatching Ulysses from a high security prison is just not on,' he warned as an afterthought. 'We shall simply have to wait: I can't imagine the FBI will simply unlock Ulysses' cell and invite him to leave, so we shall have plenty of time to consider whatever is possible.'

But Miles was mistaken. The very next day, the New York papers carried bold headlines describing the daring theft from under the very noses of the Narcotics Squad of the mysterious contents of Ulysses' crates, before anybody had a chance to examine or analyze them. How such a thing was possible would occupy the editors and commentators for days until the scandal was forgotten in the frenzy of a new story.

Ulysses was summoned from his cell and handed back his possessions by a lantern jawed police sergeant and asked to sign a receipt.

'I take it that I am free?' Ulysses enquired.

'Some friends of yours have managed to steal all the evidence which we had against you,' snapped the policeman. 'So, we can't hold you. Mind you, if I had my way –'

Ulysses interrupted before the guardian of justice had a chance to reveal what fate he would have decreed.

'You are telling me that you people have lost my crates of botanical specimens?' Ulysses demanded. 'Those heathers were a valuable collection. I shall sue the Police Department, the FBI, the New York Harbour Authority and the goddammed President himself.'

'Get your ass out of here,' snarled the cop, 'before I forget what a gentle, kindly guy I am and do you a mischief.'

Ulysses fingered a bruise which he had acquired the last time that this policeman had suffered a similar loss of memory. Deciding that he was not destined for the role of a hero, he took his leave with unceremonious haste, using a side door to avoid the attention of the press. He found the prospect of Manhattan so unappealing that he did not wait for the departure of a regular airline flight but hired a jet and hurtled away from Columbia's shores with all the celerity of one of those notorious bats out of Hell.

If Ulysses was afraid that his emergence from prison might attract the unwelcome intervention in his private life of Hiram, his concern was unfounded. Hiram and

Semiramide were far too busy to waste their time with anyone as insignificant as him. On the same morning that Ulysses slipped out of New York, they were acting as host and hostess to a most unusual gathering at the Deare Center.

Hiram's test marketing of the first small shipment of heather had been an unqualified success. The distilled nectar had lived up to his wildest claims and now that he had let it be known that commercial quantities would be available, dealers had flown into New York from all over the country. There was not a lot of them, only about a dozen, since Hiram had decided to concentrate his efforts solely on the most powerful men with the biggest purses and leave the dealing with the small fry to them. There was customarily a lot of coming and going at the Center with new patients arriving, old ones leaving and a stream of visitors and medical attendants so that a few more Cadillacs attracted no undue notice.

The satraps of the underworld assembled in one of the Center's lounges. They exchanged greetings like art dealers who were meeting at an important salesroom. The bulky, unsmiling Irishman from Boston was flanked by two bodyguards much to the amusement of the wiry black who ran Denver. Untypically, Chicago's boss was a nervous, balding man in his mid forties with pimples and steel rimmed glasses. Mr Dallas wore a cowboy's hat, the Lord of Los Angeles sported a mahogany sun-tan and the man who held New York in the palm of his hand resembled an investment banker from Wall Street.

Hiram called the meeting to order. Behind him stood the two crates, now opened and their contents visible.

'You guys know that this stuff is dynamite,' he jerked his thumb in the direction of the boxes. 'So, let's cut the bullshit and get down to business.'

'Hold it.' The speaker was a powerfully built man from Washington DC. 'We would like some assurance that this load is as potent as the samples which you sent us.'

'And it will be a pleasure for me to set your minds at rest,' Hiram oozed ingratiatingly. He grasped one of the plants from the top of the nearer crate. 'Follow me,' he invited.

He led the party into a kitchen where he proceeded to treat the plant in the way that he had been taught by Ulysses. While they waited for a small amount of nectar to be distilled, their host dispensed drinks. Semiramide flitted from one potential buyer to another, but they were not in the mood for small talk and it was with impatience that they waited for the few amber drops of liquid to be gathered in the flask. They watched carefully while Hiram poured the nectar into a glass, opened a fresh bottle of Coke and added some of the contents to the fluid. He proffered the glass to Semiramide, but Mr Washington objected.

'Not her! She's so horny all the time that we wouldn't be able to spot any difference.'

Semiramide scowled at him and was on the point of defending her tarnished honour but Hiram silenced her.

'O.K. You choose somebody. Who has brought a broad with them?'

Mr Boston got to his feet and left the room. A minute later, he returned, leading a fluffy blonde of perhaps twenty.

'She's frigid,' Mr Boston announced. He picked up the glass and handed it to the girl. 'Drink it!' he ordered.

'I ain't thirsty,' drawled the girl.

'Drink it!' repeated her swain in a voice which made it clear that this was not a subject for debate.

The girl swallowed the draught with evident distaste. 'That stuff is so acid; it's bad for my complexion.'

The men watched her expectantly. She glared back at

them, her eyes filled with resentment. Hiram addressed the Big Boss from Boston.

'Pull down your pants. It will speed up the demonstration.'

Before Mr Boston had a chance to reply, the blonde had taken matters into her own hands. She leaped on him and tore down his trousers.

'I'll show you who is frigid,' she howled.

The suddenness of her onslaught caught her prey off balance. He stumbled, tripped over a chair and sprawled onto the floor. In an instant, the avenging fury had seized his genitals and was ferociously massaging him to an erection. With a scream of triumph, she impaled herself on the prone male. The onlookers gazed in dumbfounded silence until Mr Denver broke into enthusiastic applause. One by one, the others joined in – all except the participants: Mr Boston lay there, winded and the lady was far too occupied to bother with the rest of them.

'She should be ready for two or three more of you when she has finished with him,' Hiram invited.

It took the possessed woman about ninety seconds to complete the rape of her lord and master. As Hiram had predicted, she was still unsatisfied and having dispensed with the spent body from Boston, she looked around for fresh partners.

She was not disappointed. The sight of the savage, animal sex fascinated and stimulated the men. The sinewy muscular black from Denver had dropped his trousers, revealing for the admiration of the multitude diminutive briefs which were luridly decorated by pictures of naked women. Removing his artistic pants, his long, smooth ebony penis stood proudly, beckoning the blonde who was still on her knees, astride the body of the ravished gangster. Her eyes softened and with a docility which contrasted strangely with her earlier behaviour, she took him in her mouth. The man swayed to and fro and her head followed each movement while she licked and sucked and nuzzled him.

It was an erotic entertainment and the man from Los Angeles could not wait. He saw the tremor that shook the body of Mr Denver as he pumped his seed into the avid mouth of the girl. Impatiently, he gripped her by the shoulders from behind and tipped her onto the floor. Raising her luscious rump, he plunged his thick, tightly stretched phallus into her ass and drove into her with sadistic deliberateness.

'More, more! Give me more!' breathed the formerly frigid, demure young girl. Her eyes were glassy, her voice hoarse: there could be no doubt in the minds of the men who stood around that she was totally enslaved by the lust which the tiny drop of nectar had aroused.

Mr Denver followed Mr Boston into a nearby bathroom to mop up. The other visitors stood around in a circle while the representative of Los Angeles, his hands clasped possessively over the girl's breasts, thrust into her yielding body, remorselessly, harder and harder and faster until he too came in a gushing climax which left them both breathless.

The girl was ready for yet more and a couple of the bystanders were willing to oblige, but Hiram intervened.

'O.K., boys, the show's over. If the rest of you want a broad, we can call over some cute kids who will oblige after we've completed our business. Everybody satisfied with the quality of the product?'

There was a rumble of assent. Hiram regarded the girl who had been such an ardent assistant. 'Beat it!' he said.

'But I ain't finished,' she protested.

'Oh yes you have,' Semiramide rejoined and seizing

her by the hair, lugged her out of the room. 'Go and get cleaned up!' she ordered.

'Right, gentlemen. Let's get started,' proclaimed Hiram in the tones of a mighty tycoon about to wrap up a deal. 'I am ready to sell the contents of those two crates. Cash in Switzerland, first come, first served.'

The regional bosses rallied around. Semiramide extracted bunches of heather from the large wooden boxes and exhibited them for all to see. Hiram then invited them to bid: he refused to consider any sum less than a hundred thousand dollars for each clump of the weeds. After the pantomime that they had witnessed, the visitors were keen to buy and their bidding was brisk since all of them were anxious not to be left empty handed when the whole of the stock had been sold. After an hour, all the plants had been divided into parcels and stuffed into plastic bags. Hiram's head was spinning at the prospect of the millions of dollars which were due to him and Semiramide was higher on the aroma of wealth than she had ever been on nectar or any other dope.

'Now, gentlemen,' Hiram crooned. 'If you would care to follow me into my office, my telephone is at your disposal.' He stood by with an approving smile on his lips as each of his guests called up bankers or treasurers in far off lands where they kept their snow white laundered money and instructed them to make payments to Hiram's account. Only then were they permitted to take possession of their precious purchases which they stowed away in their automobiles. After the last of them had driven away, Semiramide cast a dazzling smile at her accomplice.

'All that money! And every cent of it is ours!' she exulted.

'Not quite, honey,' Hiram amended. 'We have a payment to make tonight.'

He put through a series of calls as a result of which he was able to draw a considerable sum in dollar bills that afternoon against some of what had been credited to his account in Switzerland that morning.

That evening they celebrated, Semiramide demolishing several dozen oysters before turning her attention to a solid block of caviare. The champagne they drank may not have been the best they could have found but it certainly was the dearest. Raising her glass, Semiramide offered a toast.

'Here's to Ulysses who has made us filthy rich and never got a cent for his trouble.'

'May he rot in gaol!' Hiram added magnanimously. Neither of them had heard yet that their benefactor had been released that morning. By the time that they got back to Hiram's pad, they were delightfully drunk and on cordial terms with the universe.

'Let's go to bed,' Semiramide urged.

'Wait a little. I'm expecting some visitors,' Hiram told her.

But Semiramide did not want to wait. She did not know who Hiram's mystery callers were and she could not have cared less. Hiram had poured himself a whisky and when his back was turned, she emptied into the glass a generous measure of the honey coloured liquid she carried in the tiny bottle which she had in her bag. Half that dose, she reflected had got Ulysses going nicely.

Hiram's visitors turned out to be Mr Benson and Mr Hedges and they arrived before Hiram had time to do more than sip his drink. They regarded Semiramide with a combination of suspicion and distaste.

'What the hell are you up to?' Mr Hedges hissed conspiratorially. 'We told you to meet us alone – no witnesses, nobody to see our faces. So, what's the dame doing here?'

'Relax,' grinned Hiram, draining his glass in one gulp. 'She's O.K. She brought the stuff in.' Then, frowning at his glass, he exclaimed, 'Christ, what's the matter with this hooch! It tastes awful.'

Semiramide held her breath. She had not reckoned on giving a public performance and neither Mr Benson nor Mr Hedges seemed the type to appreciate a live sex show.

'Want a drink?' Hiram offered his guests.

Even if they had been dying of thirst, one glance at Hiram's expression would have been enough to make them sign the pledge.

'Let's get what we came here for and go,' Mr Benson replied.

Hiram produced a couple of thick piles of hundred dollar bills. The two upholders of justice counted them swiftly, stuffed them into their briefcases and prepared to depart.

'Will there be further business?' Mr Hedges asked.

'Sure! I'll let you know when we want another shipment nodded through the customs.'

'And you will remember to pay us our modest service charge, won't you?' Mr Benson uttered his request politely but firmly and Hiram could not miss the menace beneath the surface.

'Would I let you boys down?' Hiram declaimed.

Messrs Benson and Hedges regarded him sceptically and left the room without another word, clutching their bulging briefcases.

'I wouldn't like to get on the wrong side of those boys,' observed Hiram. 'Say, honey, what's got into you?'

Semiramide was gazing at him, her eyes wide with astonishment.

'Hiram, don't you feel anything?'

'What are you talking about? I feel rich – isn't that good enough?'

'I mean feel something for me,' Semiramide said. 'Why, hell, you don't even have an erection!'

'All in good time,' smiled Hiram. 'I think I'll have a coffee to take the taste of that whisky out of my mouth. God, it was foul! Then, we can go to bed. I'll even take my socks off tonight for you.'

Fear gripped Semiramide. 'Listen, maybe that nectar doesn't work on everybody. You see, I put a shot of the stuff you gave me into your Scotch and it hasn't got through to you. Hiram, do you think that some people are immune?'

Hiram considered the problem. 'Tell me,' he said thoughtfully, 'did you use any of it on Ulysses?'

Semiramide nodded.

'Well,' Hiram laughed, 'I guess that he spotted where you kept the juice and doctored it in case you gave him a repeat dose. He's got a cunning streak, our Ulysses: he surely fooled you.'

Semiramide did not share Hiram's amusement. If Ulysses was capable of playing one trick on them, maybe he had left them other booby traps. But Hiram's confidence and good humour were so infectious that gradually her suspicions were allayed.

Hiram was as good as his word. Having drunk a cup of coffee, he prepared for bed and had removed his socks when the phone rang.

'Leave it,' called Semiramide who was already comfortably snuggling in bed.

But there is something imperative about a phone ringing in the middle of the night and Hiram could not ignore its summons.

The caller was the tough customer who held the

franchize for Washington. He went straight to the point.

'I'm coming back to New York tomorrow, you punk,' he bellowed, 'and I shall tear you apart, limb from limb. Then, I shall scatter fragments of your unsavoury body in each of the States of the Union.'

'Say, man, what's got into you?' demanded the flabbergasted Hiram.

'You know darned well,' retorted his caller. 'That heather you gave me is phoney.'

'Baloney!' Hiram shouted. 'You saw the way the stuff worked. Have you set up your still right?'

'I saw how some other heather worked,' contradicted Mr Washington DC. 'You worked a switcharoo. I'm coming for you, Hiram, boy.'

Before Hiram could argue, he had hung up. Maybe he ought to have given a few more demonstrations, not of the effect of nectar, but on the practicalities of installing and operating a mini-distillery. Moodily, Hiram got into bed. As he turned towards Semiramide, the phone shrilled again.

This time, the nice, mild tempered man from Chicago advised him to write his will. By the time he had been abused by Denver and threatened anew from Los Angeles, Hiram was reduced to a nervous stammering, sweating wreck.

'What are you going to do?' Semiramide asked. 'Are you thinking of giving the boys their money back?'

Hiram shook his head. 'They want the goods. And can you imagine those two sharks from the Narcotics Squad handing back those great bundles of lovely money? No, tell me, do you know exactly where Ulysses got the heather? We are certain that the stuff on top of the crates was good. If we can get more of those to replace the bad plants, I should be able to straighten out the customers.'

'Don't worry,' Semiramide smiled grimly. 'That Ulysses dragged me through every blasted field and common in Britain. I've seen all the heathers that God Almighty ever created.'

'What's the good of that,' Hiram exclaimed impatiently, 'unless you know the precise spot where each one was found.'

'But I do,' Semiramide told him triumphantly. 'When we were trekking all over the country, Ulysses kept a map and he carefully marked every location together with a description of the plants we found there. I reckoned with our having arranged for him to retire from the business, that map would be more use to me than to him, so I lifted it from him when we hit New York. Look, I'll show you.'

She climbed out of bed and went over to a writing desk from which she produced a large, carefully marked map of the United Kingdom.

Hiram sighed with relief. 'You're a clever girl. Tomorrow morning we fly to England.'

Again the phone rang. Reluctantly, Hiram took the call. This time, he said nothing, only listened, grew pale and replaced the receiver.

'Quick,' he told Semiramide, 'get dressed and packed. I reckon we have less than fifteen minutes to get out.'

'But you said we would go in the morning,' she protested.

'We've no time. That was the boy from New York. He and some of his friends are on their way round.'

Ten minutes, twenty-five seconds later, the door slammed behind them. They had thrown the bare necessities into a suitcase, grabbed their money, passports and the precious heather map and were now heading for the airport. They dared not risk waiting for a flight out, so like Ulysses not many hours before them, they hired a jet so as to get clear before their pursuers caught up with them.

In the various cities of the United States, gangsters turned amateur chemists were looking with disgust at the revolting mass of shrivelled brown heather debris which clogged their hastily assembled distilleries. Their fumes had polluted the atmosphere, thick, heavy and oily. As for the distillate, their efforts had been rewarded by a trickle of bitter, brackish liquid, the aphrodisiac effects of which were comparable with those of the cold tea which Semiramide had administered to Hiram. But, as they settled back in the cabin of the plane, the two fugitives were not concerned with such trifles as the ecology of America: they were entirely preoccupied with saving their own skins.

Meanwhile, Ulysses had preceded them into London. He had checked into a small, unobtrusive hotel and from there, he had called Lucinda. He apologized that he did not have the time to pay another visit to Hamblewood during this trip but he requested his niece to come to his hotel without delay. So, while Hiram and Semiramide were racing across the Atlantic, Lucinda and Brian were sitting in the back of the lobby of the hotel, which served as a lounge, listening to Ulysses' account of recent events.

'But won't Hiram be coming after you?' Brian asked.

'I guess so, but I don't think that he will find me,' answered Ulysses.

Brian persisted. 'Surely a crook like him will have contacts in England? They'll hunt you down, even in a small, out of the way hotel like this one.'

'I'm not reckoning on staying around for many days,' Ulysses assured him, 'and I hope that my Bulgarian passport might confuse them for a while.'

'You have a Bulgarian passport?'

'Yes, indeed, Brian. It seemed a sensible precaution to buy one.'

'But you don't speak Bulgarian,' Lucinda objected.

'And do you think that anybody else in a sleepy hotel in the middle of nowhere speaks Bulgarian?' her uncle replied. 'The dumb thing would have been to buy a phoney French or German passport – but Bulgarian, who is going to chat to me in my supposed native tongue?'

'Didn't the reception clerk wonder how you came to find this hotel?' Lucinda enquired.

'Of course he did. I told him I had been recommended to come here by Krassov at the embassy.'

'And is there a Krassov at the Bulgarian embassy?' Brian wanted to know.

'I don't suppose so,' Ulysses said, 'but they won't ask. They will assume that I mistook the name of the hotel and, since I paid in advance, will be happy enough.'

'You've got it all worked out, haven't you?' Lucinda asked admiringly. 'We were so worried when we saw you on TV. I persuaded Brian to stay on at Hamblewood so that we could go together to the States to help you. But I honestly had no idea what we could have done.'

'I appreciate your concern,' Ulysses told her, 'but there is something that you could do now. It means putting you to some trouble, but I can pay you well for your pains.'

'Just say the word,' Lucinda assured him.

'Well, the Bulgarian passport is fine for getting me in or out of the country but it would be good for my health to drop out of sight for a while. In a place like London, there is always the possibility of being seen by chance and, pretty soon, the word gets out. I need a vacation somewhere nobody ever goes. How about my chartering your boat, smuggling myself aboard and having you sail me back to dear, old Xanthos? Hiram's hoodlums don't even know the place exists: I'd be perfectly safe there.'

'Great!' exclaimed Lucinda. 'I was going to suggest just that. And you don't have to worry about chartering Lucifer. We were intending to take her back to Xanthos ourselves, weren't we, Brian?'

'Were we?' Brian asked. It was the first he had heard of the scheme.

'You know we were. We don't have any of the heather left. Miles gave the last of it to you, didn't he?'

Ulysses nodded assent.

'We, that is I,' Lucinda amended, 'thought that we should build up our stocks again. Perhaps we could market it in the States.'

'That is a course which I would not recommend at this time,' her uncle warned. 'But if you are going to sail to Xanthos, it would be most convenient for me to be a stowaway. How soon could we get started?'

'What do you think, Brian?' Lucinda asked. 'You're not going to slink off home now when you are needed, are you?'

Brian did not hesitate. Things had not been too good between them during the past few days but that was at Hamblewood, with the formalities of the Farrer's family life, and they had been concerned about the fate of Ulysses. It would be different on board Lucifer, away from all the strains and tensions. He remembered those days together, and the nights in Lucinda's cabin. Furthermore, he considered that her short lived but passionate affair with Paul would recede into a nostalgic memory quicker and more painlessly afloat.

'We know that Alain has finished fitting her out after our last trip, so he ought to be ready to put to sea whenever we want. Clearing up here shouldn't take us more than a couple of days.'

'Fine,' said Ulysses. 'If you will allow me, I shall go on ahead and get on board, out of the sight of any of my possibly inquisitive acquaintances.'

They took their leave of their Bulgarian friend who hurried to make the necessary arrangements for his journey to La Napoule. Lucinda kissed Brian fondly.

'It was good of you to scrap your plans for going home and help out,' she said.

'This could be fun,' Brian smiled. 'Anyway, it would be no time to desert ship. Now, hadn't you better phone Alain and Jennifer and let them know that we are putting to sea?'

The news that Lucinda was once more going off on her travels was met with cool unconcern by her mother and positive satisfaction by her father who had practically forgotten that their recent predicament had been the result of his own gullibility and was not the consequence of some lapse of his daughter. Life without her would be more tranquil, her father judged.

So, a few days later, the ketch, Lucifer, nosed her way out of the harbour entrance into the open sea. Alain stood at the wheel with Jennifer beside him. Ulysses, who had remained below while preparations for the voyage had been completed, had emerged and was enjoying the quickening breeze. He looked suitably piratical, with his pointed, grey beard and alert blue eyes, as he gazed with amusement mingled with defiance at the receding coastline.

Once clear of the harbour, Alain cut the motor and he and Jennifer set about hoisting the sails.

'Where the hell are Brian and Lucinda?' Alain demanded angrily. 'They ought to be up here, giving a hand.'

'You should know by now that when they vanish Lucinda

is celebrating certain rites of passage with her man,' Jennifer told him. 'Don't disturb them: we can manage quite well on our own.'

'It's like being home again,' Lucinda murmured happily as she and Brian stretched out in their bed in the owners' cabin.

'Shouldn't we go up and give the others a hand?' Brian suggested tentatively.

'Kiss me and stop asking silly questions,' Lucinda commanded.

Brian complied willingly. After all, the other two would have their turn later and, if necessary, Ulysses could help on deck for a while.

He took Lucinda in his arms and held her tight. There was something reassuring about making love to her in the familiar surroundings of 'Lucifer'. They had enjoyed so many good times together in that cabin and been so contented with each other before Lucinda had met Paul.

The thought of his formidable rival worried Brian. How could he be sure that Lucinda was not thinking about Paul and missing him even while she lay in Brian's arms? At that moment, Brian was haunted by the memory of how easy and satisfying had been their sex in those days and nights before they had even known of Paul's existence. What a contrast with the strains and tensions which had grown up subsequently!

How would it work out this time? How would he be able to make love to Lucinda with the shadow of Paul lying across their bed?

'What's the matter?' asked Lucinda. 'Don't you feel like it?'

Brian smiled feebly. He wanted her wildly, as much as ever before but not merely as Paul's surrogate. The thought flashed across his mind – if only I could make marvellous, passionate love and sweep her off her feet and exorcise for ever that spectre from the past.

But could he do it? He was racked by anxiety, and anxiety never makes for good sex.

Lucinda stretched invitingly those long, slender legs which he adored: Brian was torn between lust and doubt.

'I want you to take my breast and fondle it, kiss it, suck it, lick it,' coaxed Lucinda. Then she exploded, 'Christ, what's got into you? I've never had to spell it out for you before. You're too young for the menopause or have you fallen for some other pretty chick? It's not Jennifer, is it?'

'No, there's nothing like that,' Brian hastily assured her.

More to placate her suspicions than to satisfy his own erotic impulse, Brian took the proffered breast in his mouth and started to play his tongue around her delectable tit. However, the sensation of that seductive flesh soon dispelled his misery. It stiffened his resolve and also the most relevant part of his body. He held her and stroked and caressed her as if he were discovering her beauty for the first time. Yet, at the back of his mind that nagging doubt persisted and Lucinda sensed that something was wrong. He knew that there was no way he could satisfy Lucinda or find satisfaction himself without bringing it into the open.

With a feigned casualness, Brian asked, 'Do you think that you will hear from Paul again?'

'Is that what's bugging you,' Lucinda replied. 'Why should I? He has his own life and I have mine. We had a good time but he doesn't need me and I don't need him. And unless you snap out of it, I won't need you either.'

It was over. The tension had passed. Brian felt as if his virility had been restored to him.

'It's good to be back,' he said and he enjoyed a newly

rediscovered contentment as he felt Lucinda responding to his caresses with her old warmth.

As for Lucinda, she realized with a glow of pleasure just how well attuned Brian had become to her ways. Together they made the sweet music of love, totally absorbed in the perfection of their bodies. His arms encircled her, strong, firm flesh against her softness. His scent tingled her nostrils, his tongue possessed her mouth and the faint bristles of his chin and cheeks rubbed against her face. Everything about him was desirable and comfortingly familiar. Without her saying a word, he seemed to know exactly where she wanted him to touch her, when to whisper words of love and when to be silent, when to change position, when to strain and when to relax, when to dominate and when to submit. She would never tire of his potent masculinity. He was the man who could make her feel the complete woman and this encounter, like those in the past and others which still lay in the future, was a wonderful experience, and like them, it was something unique.

Her orgasm brought her the calm of complete fulfilment. As she lay back and Brian slowly stroked her face, her shoulders, her breasts, she felt radiantly happy. What more could a woman want?

'This is where you belong,' Brian said with quiet assurance, 'always!'

She kissed him tenderly, but she did not reply. Maybe it was true, as Brian had contended for so long, that they were so suited to each other, so well matched, that she would not need any other man for the rest of her active life. But, deep inside her, there was a voice which denied this fairy tale ending. Even if she never needed another man, it told her, she would crave fresh adventures and some other lovers would spark off desire in her mind and body. She knew that she loved Brian but that voice told her there would be others and that she had not been designed by Fate to be some man's constant companion and faithful mate, renouncing all others. After all, she told herself, I adore strawberries, but that doesn't prevent me from eating and enjoying other fruit.

But, for the present, Brian was the man in her life. How long would that last? That was another matter, she thought with a smile.

Epilogue

Viscountess Hamblewood was displeased. She put down the morning newspaper which contained the story which had offended her.

'You would think that foreigners, coming to England, would behave themselves,' she pontificated.

Viscount Hamblewood thought that, as his wife had been born and bred in the United States, her statement was a little odd, but he considered it would be tactless to voice his observation.

'Not only did this couple show a disgusting lack of respect,' continued Melanie, 'but they are undoubtedly completely dotty.'

'If you say so, my dear,' assented Gerald, who had not the faintest idea what she was talking about.

He picked up the paper and emitted a startled bray. There, staring at him, like a brace of accusing angels from his guilty past, were the likenesses of Hiram and Semiramide. The caption beneath the picture gave them other names, but Gerald knew them for who they were.

'What's the matter?' asked Melanie. 'Do you know those people, Gerald?'

'No, oh no, not at all,' he hurriedly assured her. 'I just had a twinge – rheumatism or gout or something.'

Melanie regarded him with her habitual frosty suspicion but her husband bestowed on her a watery smile of inane innocence. With a sniff, Melanie rose and left the breakfast room to go and persecute the kitchen staff.

As soon as he was satisfied that his wife was not waiting

outside the door to pounce on him, Gerald eagerly read the news item which accompanied the photograph of his former companions.

That the two were back in England sent a tremor down his spine. However, it was unlikely that they would intrude once more on the ordered routine of life at Hamblewood since they were safely in the custody of the police.

The circumstances which had led to Hiram and Semiramide being detained were certainly unusual. All sorts of felons have been discovered from time to time trespassing in unlikely places but what, the reporter wondered, could have induced this couple who had apparently only a few hours previously arrived from the United States to break into the grounds of the country residence of the Queen at Sandringham. It did not look as if they planned to commit a robbery since the only implements they had brought with them were a couple of brand new garden spades.

Nor was it likely that they were pursuing some wild notion that there was treasure buried on the estate for, when they were apprehended, at one o'clock in the morning, they were working like demons, digging up great clumps of heather which they were stuffing into sacks. They had in their possession, it was noted, a map on which several sites, including Sandringham, had been marked, but the police were unable to deduce the significance of these locations, most of which were in wild country or common land.

It was also reported that the two intruders would be examined by psychiatrists. The man, on being questioned by the police, had been anxious to confess his guilt, not only of trespass but of every crime and misdemeanour imaginable, and he pleaded with the authorities to convict him and sentence him to the maximum term of imprisonment. 'A life stretch in a high security prison in Britain,' Hiram was reported as saying, 'would be doing me a favour.'

It is possible that if the trespassers are not found to be suffering from some mental disorder, the Home Office might consider them to be undesirable visitors to this country and order them to be deported back to the United States. Such was the concluding paragraph of the item.